A WORD A DAY
A DAY GRADE 1

Editorial Development: Marilyn Evans
Robyn Raymer
Sarita Chávez
Silverman
Susan Rose Simms
Copy Editing: Carrie Gwynne
Art Direction: Cheryl Puckett
Cover Design: David Price
Design/Production: Susan Bigger
John D. Williams

EMC 2791

Evan-Moor
EDUCATIONAL PUBLISHERS
Helping Children Learn since 1979

Congratulations on your purchase of some of the finest teaching materials in the world.

Correlated to State Standards

Photocopying the pages in this book is permitted for <u>single-classroom use only</u>. Making photocopies for additional classes or schools is prohibited.

For information about other Evan-Moor products, call 1-800-777-4362, fax 1-800-777-4332, or visit our Web site, www.evan-moor.com. Entire contents © 2009 EVAN-MOOR CORP. 18 Lower Ragsdale Drive, Monterey, CA 93940-5746. Printed in USA.

Visit *teaching-standards.com* to view a correlation of this book's activities to your state's standards. This is a free service.

Weekly Walk-Through

Each week of **A Word a Day** follows the same format,
making it easy for both students and teacher to use.

Words of the Week

Four new words are presented each week. A definition, example sentence, and discussion prompts are provided for each word.

Part of Speech The part of speech is identified. You may or may not want to share this information with the class, depending on the skill level of your students.

Example Sentence Each new word is used in a sentence designed to provide enough context for students to easily grasp its meaning. The same sentence is found in the reproducible student dictionary, which begins on page 148.

Critical Attributes Prompt Discussion questions are provided that require students to identify features that are and are not attributes of the target word. This is one of the most effective ways to help students recognize subtleties of meaning.

Definition
Each word is defined in a complete sentence. The same definition is found in the reproducible student dictionary, which begins on page 148.

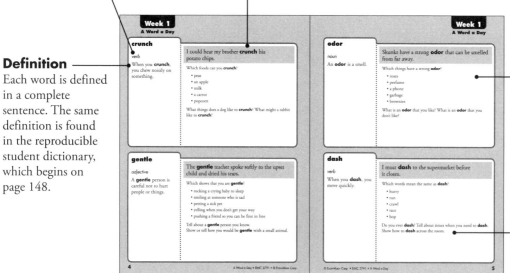

Personal Connection Prompt Students are asked to share an opinion, an idea, or a personal experience that demonstrates their understanding of the new word.

How to Present the Words

Use one of the following methods to present each word:

- Write the word on the board. Then read the definition and the example sentence, explaining as needed before conducting oral activities.

- Make an overhead transparency of the lesson page that shows the word. Then guide students through the definition, example sentence, and oral activities.

- Reproduce the dictionary on pages 148–159 for each student, or provide each student with a student practice book. (See inside front cover.) Have students find the word in their dictionaries, and then guide them through the definition, example sentence, and oral activities.

End-of-Week Review

Review the four words of the week through oral and written activities designed to reinforce student understanding.

Oral Review

Four oral activities provide you with prompts to review the week's words.

Written Assessment

A student reproducible containing four multiple-choice items and an open-ended writing activity can be used to assess students' mastery.

Additional Features

- Reproducible student dictionary
- Cumulative word index

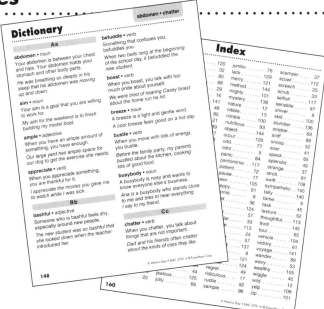

crunch

verb

When you **crunch**, you chew noisily on something.

I could hear my brother **crunch** his potato chips.

Which foods can you **crunch**?

- peas
- an apple
- milk
- a carrot
- popcorn

What things does a dog like to **crunch**? What might a rabbit like to **crunch**?

gentle

adjective

A **gentle** person is careful not to hurt people or things.

The **gentle** teacher spoke softly to the upset child and dried his tears.

Which shows that you are **gentle**?

- rocking a crying baby to sleep
- smiling at someone who is sad
- petting a sick pet
- yelling when you don't get your way
- pushing a friend so you can be first in line

Tell about a **gentle** person you know.
Show or tell how you would be **gentle** with a small animal.

odor

noun

An **odor** is a smell.

Skunks have a strong **odor** that can be smelled from far away.

Which things have a strong **odor**?

- roses
- perfume
- a phone
- garbage
- brownies

What is an **odor** that you like? What is an **odor** that you don't like?

dash

verb

When you **dash**, you move quickly.

I must **dash** to the supermarket before it closes.

Which words mean the same as **dash**?

- hurry
- run
- crawl
- race
- hop

Do you ever **dash**? Tell about times when you need to **dash**. Show how to **dash** across the room.

crunch • gentle • odor • dash

Write on the board the four words studied this week. Read the words with the class and briefly review their meanings. Then conduct the oral activities below.

1 Tell students that you are going to give them a clue about one of the words for the week. They are to find the word that answers the clue.

- This word describes someone who is kind and not rough. **(gentle)**

- You would do this in a race. **(dash)**

- You might do this when you eat cereal. **(crunch)**

- You might notice this in a flower garden. **(an odor)**

2 Read each sentence and ask students to supply the correct word to complete the sentence.

- I like the ____ of fresh brownies. **(odor)**

- The ____ man did not yell when I accidentally broke his window. **(gentle)**

- Molly is hurt. Please ____ to the nurse and ask her to come. **(dash)**

- I like the sound I make when I ____ pretzels. **(crunch)**

3 Read each sentence and ask students to tell which word or words are wrong. Then have them provide the correct word from the week's list.

- I slurp popcorn when I'm at the movies. **(slurp/crunch)**

- The mean child hugged the little girl who was crying. **(mean/gentle)**

- A stinky sound came from the pile of trash. **(sound/odor)**

- Be sure to run slowly so you will win the race. **(run slowly/dash)**

4 Read each sentence and ask students to decide if it is true or false. If the sentence is false, instruct students to explain why.

- Firefighters dash to put out fires. **(true)**

- A gentle person often yells and screams at people. **(false; a gentle person is kind and talks quietly)**

- An odor is something you can see. **(false; an odor is something you smell)**

- You make noises when you crunch food. **(true)**

Answers for page 7: 1. A, 2. G, 3. D, 4. H

Review Words   crunch • gentle • odor • dash

Fill in the bubble next to the correct answer.

1. Which sentence uses the word *odor* correctly?
- Ⓐ I like the odor of hot dogs cooking on a grill.
- Ⓑ My room has red odor on the walls.
- Ⓒ Emma made a large odor out of wood.
- Ⓓ What odor should I put on the cookie?

2. When you *dash*, you ___.
- Ⓕ walk slowly
- Ⓖ move quickly
- Ⓗ read quietly
- Ⓙ speak loudly

3. The word *crunch* tells the way someone ___.
- Ⓐ laughs
- Ⓑ sleeps
- Ⓒ sings
- Ⓓ chews

4. Which sentence tells about a *gentle* person?
- Ⓕ Jonathan kicked sand in his little brother's face.
- Ⓖ Rosa threw her baseball glove to scare her cat.
- Ⓗ Grandma smiled lovingly at Ben and patted his hand.
- Ⓙ Kate pushed to be first in line and made her friends mad.

Writing

Write about an odor you like. Use **odor** in your sentence.

_____

_____

shiver

verb

When you **shiver**, you shake because you are cold or afraid.

When I got out of the swimming pool, the cold wind made me **shiver**.

Which of these could make you **shiver**?

- kicking off the blankets on a cold night
- sitting in front of a fireplace
- hearing creaky sounds on the roof
- jumping into a cold lake
- curling up with a good book

What do your teeth do when you **shiver**? What happens to your skin when you **shiver**?
Show what it's like to **shiver**.

racket

noun

A **racket** is a lot of very loud noise.

The squawking birds in the pet store made an awful **racket**.

Which of these would make a **racket**?

- a dripping faucet
- children yelling at a ballgame
- a stack of pots and pans falling over
- a goldfish swimming in a bowl
- three dogs barking at a cat

In what kind of place is it all right to make a **racket**?
Where is it not okay to make a **racket**?

tame

adjective

Something that is **tame** is gentle and not wild.

The **tame** deer were not afraid to be near us.

Which are **tame** animals?

- a pet cat
- a wolf
- a zebra
- a grizzly bear
- a pet dog

Tell about some **tame** animals you have seen.
What can you do with a **tame** animal that you cannot do with a wild animal?

permit

verb

You **permit** something when you allow it to happen.

Will you **permit** me to go to the beach with Sam and his family?

Pretend you are a parent. Which things would you **permit** your first-grader to do?

- go trick-or-treating
- have a pet
- jump from an airplane
- drive a car
- play on a sports team

Think about a time when you asked your mom or dad to **permit** you to do something. What did you say? What did your mom or dad say?

shiver • racket • tame • permit

Write on the board the four words studied this week. Read the words with the class and briefly review their meanings. Then conduct the oral activities below.

1 Tell students that you are going to give them a clue about one of the words for the week. They are to find the word that answers the clue.

- You might do this when you're very cold. (**shiver**)

- A pet cat is this kind of animal. (**tame**)

- Your teacher might do this when you ask to leave the classroom. (**permit you to leave**)

- If a lot of people were beating on drums, you might call it this. (**a racket**)

2 Read each sentence and ask students to supply the correct word to complete the sentence.

- My mom said she will ___ me to go on the school trip. (**permit**)

- The metal trash cans made a ___ when the wind knocked them over. (**racket**)

- The scary part of the movie made me ___. (**shiver**)

- The ___ bird ate seeds from my hand. (**tame**)

3 Read each sentence and ask students to tell which word or words are wrong. Then have them provide the correct word from the week's list.

- A helicopter makes a soft sound when it takes off. (**soft sound/racket**)

- My puppy is a wild animal that sleeps on my bed. (**wild/tame**)

- Dad said, "Yes, I will not allow you to go to the ballgame." (**not allow/permit**)

- I began to sweat because I was very cold. (**sweat/shiver**)

4 Read each sentence and ask students to decide if it is true or false. If the sentence is false, instruct students to explain why.

- When you shiver, you might also get goose bumps. (**true**)

- Snow makes a racket as it falls on the ground. (**false; snow falls quietly**)

- A tiger is a tame animal that can live in your yard. (**false; a tiger is dangerous and lives in the wild**)

- The word *permit* means about the same as *allow*. (**true**)

Answers for page 11: 1. B, 2. F, 3. C, 4. J

Fill in the bubble next to the correct answer.

1. Which sentence uses the word *racket* correctly?

Ⓐ I will racket your mother to ask if you can come to my house.

Ⓑ Some monkeys made a racket in the trees.

Ⓒ My sheet of paper made a racket when it fell on the floor.

Ⓓ Please racket me when you get home.

2. When you *permit* something, you ___ .

Ⓕ let it happen

Ⓖ stop it from happening

Ⓗ wish it would happen

Ⓙ wonder if it will happen

3. Which might make you *shiver*?

Ⓐ riding your bike on a sunny day

Ⓑ baking cookies with your mom

Ⓒ walking on a cold, windy day without your jacket

Ⓓ watching funny cartoons about talking animals

4. Which tells about a *tame* animal?

Ⓕ A bears lives in the forest.

Ⓖ A lion hunts for its food.

Ⓗ A snake can be dangerous.

Ⓙ My dog likes to play ball with me.

| Writing |

Write about something that makes a racket. Use **racket** in your sentence.

_____

_____

nature

noun

Nature is everything in the world that is not made by people, such as trees, rocks, and animals.

Our drive through the forest gave us a chance to enjoy the beauty of **nature**.

Which are things you can do in **nature**?

- camp in a forest
- grow a flower garden
- ride in an elevator
- go fishing in a pond
- watch a spider spin a web

Name things that are found in **nature**. Make a list and see how long the list will be.
What are some ways you enjoy **nature**?

wild

adjective

A **wild** animal is not tame and lives in nature.

A lion is a **wild** animal that lives on grasslands and hunts for its food.

Which animals are **wild**?

- a kitten in a pet shop
- a monkey in a tree
- a bat in a cave
- a tiger in a jungle
- a shark in the ocean

Tell what you know about one **wild** animal. What sound does that **wild** animal make?

nibble

verb

You **nibble** your food when you eat it in small bites.

My pet mouse **nibbled** on a piece of cheese.

Which ones might **nibble**?

- a wolf eating its prey
- a queen eating a cookie
- a person in a pie-eating contest
- a child tasting a new food
- a bear with a fish

Pretend you are holding a slice of pizza. Show how you would **nibble** it.

What is your favorite food to **nibble**?

focus

verb

You **focus** when you pay attention.

Lucy could not **focus** on her homework because her brother was playing loud music.

When are good times to **focus**?

- when your teacher is talking
- when you read
- when you are playing a game
- when you are walking on the beach
- when you sleep

What helps you to **focus** in school? What makes it difficult for you to **focus**?

nature • wild • nibble • focus

Write on the board the four words studied this week. Read the words with the class and briefly review their meanings. Then conduct the oral activities below.

1 Tell students that you are going to give them a clue about one of the words for the week. They are to find the word that answers the clue.

- You need to do this when you read. (**focus**)

- Tigers and eagles are this kind of animal. (**wild**)

- A rabbit might do this when it eats lettuce. (**nibble**)

- Plants, rocks, and animals are all part of this. (**nature**)

2 Read each sentence and ask students to supply the correct word to complete the sentence.

- An elephant is the largest ____ animal that lives on land. (**wild**)

- A mouse likes to ____ on seeds. (**nibble**)

- One way to protect ____ is to throw trash in containers. (**nature**)

- I ____ on the screen when I watch a movie. (**focus**)

3 Read each sentence and ask students to tell which word or words are wrong. Then have them provide the correct word from the week's list.

- Rats drink their food in small bites. (**drink/nibble**)

- I look down when my teacher writes on the board. (**look down/focus**)

- An alligator is a tame animal with rows of sharp teeth. (**tame/wild**)

- I love to camp in the city where wild animals live. (**the city/nature**)

4 Read each sentence and ask students to decide if it is true or false. If the sentence is false, instruct students to explain why.

- A polar bear is a wild animal. (**true**)

- Schools are part of nature. (**false; people make school buildings**)

- It is important to focus when you do your homework. (**true**)

- Lions nibble their food with their big teeth. (**false; lions take big bites of their food**)

Answers for page 15: 1. B, 2. G, 3. A, 4. F

| Review Words | nature • wild • nibble • focus |

Fill in the bubble next to the correct answer.

1. Which sentence uses the word *nature* correctly?
- Ⓐ Will you nature up the tree and pick an apple for me?
- Ⓑ The water you drink comes from nature.
- Ⓒ Airplanes are my favorite part of nature.
- Ⓓ Nature makes computers and televisions.

2. Which is a *wild* animal?
- Ⓕ a horse carrying a rider
- Ⓖ a bird making a nest
- Ⓗ a cat sleeping on a person's lap
- Ⓙ a dog walking on a leash

3. When you *focus* on what someone is saying, you ___ .
- Ⓐ listen carefully
- Ⓑ sing a song
- Ⓒ daydream
- Ⓓ turn on a light

4. When you *nibble* your food, you ___ .
- Ⓕ take small bites
- Ⓖ open wide and take a big bite
- Ⓗ chew as loudly as you can
- Ⓙ drink with a straw

| Writing |

Write about a way to take care of nature. Use **nature** in your sentence.

_____

_____

favor

noun

A **favor** is something nice that you do for another person.

The busy teacher said, "Please do me a **favor** and pass out the pencils."

Which of these actions are **favors**?

- You offer to play with the baby while Mom makes dinner.
- You ask your teacher if he needs help.
- You pretend not to hear your dad when he tells you it's time for bed.
- You offer to help your sister learn to play a game.
- You put on your pajamas before you go to sleep.

Tell about a **favor** that someone did for you. Tell about a **favor** that you did for someone.

giggle

verb

When you **giggle**, you laugh in a silly or nervous way.

The girls at the sleepover **giggled** as they put makeup on each other.

When is a time to **giggle**?

- when you hear a joke
- when you are taking a test
- when your friend is sad
- when someone tickles you
- when you watch a cartoon

Have you ever started to **giggle** and could not stop? Where were you and what happened?

pause

verb

You **pause** when you stop what you are doing for a short time.

Let's **pause** for lunch and then finish our work when we come back.

Which might make you **pause**?

- feeling very thirsty during a ballgame
- reading a very funny story
- seeing a beautiful rosebush while you are walking
- listening to important news
- hearing a sudden loud noise while you are doing your homework

What are some reasons for **pausing** during a school day?

ridiculous

adjective

Something that is very silly is **ridiculous**.

It would be **ridiculous** to wear polka-dotted pajamas to school.

Which are **ridiculous** ways to behave?

- sticking a hot dog in your ear
- washing your hands before you eat
- walking backward all day
- wearing your shoes on your ears
- zipping your jacket when it's cold

What is the most **ridiculous** thing you've ever seen? Tell why you think it was **ridiculous**.

favor • giggle • pause • ridiculous

Write on the board the four words studied this week. Read the words with the class and briefly review their meanings. Then conduct the oral activities below.

1 Tell students that you are going to give them a clue about one of the words for the week. They are to find the word that answers the clue.

- This word describes something that is very silly. (**ridiculous**)

- You might do this when you see something that is ridiculous. (**giggle**)

- You might do this for someone who needs help. (**a favor**)

- When you do this, you take a short break from what you are doing. (**pause**)

2 Read each sentence and ask students to supply the correct word to complete the sentence.

- As she reads, our teacher likes to ____ to ask us questions about the story. (**pause**)

- I wrote a ____ story about a dancing pig that wears a wig. (**ridiculous**)

- Jenny began to ____ as she watched the monkeys play at the zoo. (**giggle**)

- Please do me a ____ and pick up the book that I dropped. (**favor**)

3 Read each sentence and ask students to tell which word or words are wrong. Then have them provide the correct word from the week's list.

- I can hear Rosa cry as she watches cartoons. (**cry/giggle**)

- Putting your dress on your dog is a wise thing to do. (**wise/ridiculous**)

- Please keep working if you need a break. (**keep working/pause**)

- Thanks so much for your help—I really appreciate the mean trick. (**mean trick/favor**)

4 Read each sentence and ask students to decide if it is true or false. If the sentence is false, instruct students to explain why.

- You are doing your neighbor a favor when you offer to walk her dog. (**true**)

- It is good to pause and think before answering a question. (**true**)

- It would be ridiculous for a cat to wear a necklace and earrings. (**true**)

- It is okay to giggle at a friend who feels sad. (**false; you should be kind to a sad friend, not laugh at him or her**)

Answers for page 19: 1. C, 2. J, 3. A, 4. G

Review Words	favor • giggle • pause • ridiculous

Fill in the bubble next to the correct answer.

1. Which sentence uses the word *favor* correctly?
   Ⓐ I favor and giggle when I hear a good joke.
   Ⓑ I did my sister a favor when I made fun of her.
   Ⓒ I can do you a favor and help you carry the bags.
   Ⓓ Only a selfish person would do a favor like that.

2. Which sentence tells of a *ridiculous* thing to do?
   Ⓕ I brush my teeth after I eat.
   Ⓖ I raise my hand in class when I want to give an answer.
   Ⓗ I wash up before I go to bed.
   Ⓙ I put on my pajamas when I wake up in the morning.

3. If you heard some kids *giggle*, you would probably ____.
   Ⓐ wonder what was funny
   Ⓑ wonder why the kids felt sad
   Ⓒ wonder why the kids were mad
   Ⓓ wonder why the kids felt scared

4. When you *pause*, you ____.
   Ⓕ keep going without a break
   Ⓖ stop for a short time
   Ⓗ start all over again
   Ⓙ stop for a long time

Writing

Write about something that makes you giggle. Use **giggle** in your sentence.

_____

_____

hero

noun

A **hero** is a person who does a brave and good thing.

That firefighter is the **hero** who saved the boy from the burning house.

Which of these people are **heroes**?

- a person who calls 911 in an emergency
- a girl who puts her toys away
- a boy who helps his dad make lunch
- a woman who saves a drowning child
- a farmer who grows corn

Pretend you are a **hero** who did something good and brave. Tell why you are a **hero**.

dull

adjective

Something that is **dull** is boring.

Harry thinks books without pictures are **dull**.

Which of these activities seem **dull** to you?

- riding in a fire engine
- pulling weeds in a garden
- going on rides at a fair
- playing a computer game
- listening to a long speech

Do you do any chores that are **dull**? What **dull** chores do you do? How can you change a **dull** chore into one that is more fun?

create

verb

You **create** something when you make it from your own ideas.

I want to **create** a puppet using paper plates, colored paper, crayons, and glue.

What might you **create** with each group of things?

- easel, paints, paintbrushes
- wood, nails, hammer
- yarn, noodles, paints
- colored tissue paper, buttons, paper tube, string
- colored, paper, marking pens, scissors

What things do you like to use when you **create**?
What is something you **created** that you are proud of?

firm

adjective

A **firm** object is hard and solid.

I know that this apple is **firm** because it feels hard when I press my thumb on it.

Which objects are **firm**?

- a soft pillow
- water
- orange juice
- a baseball
- a wooden chair

Look around the classroom and name objects that are **firm**.

hero • dull • create • firm

Write on the board the four words studied this week. Read the words with the class and briefly review their meanings. Then conduct the oral activities below.

1 Tell students that you are going to give them a clue about one of the words for the week. They are to find the word that answers the clue.

- You do this when you make something from your own ideas. (**create**)

- This word describes something that isn't fun or exciting. (**dull**)

- A dog could be one if it saved someone's life. (**a hero**)

- This word describes something that is hard when you touch it. (**firm**)

2 Read each sentence and ask students to supply the correct word to complete the sentence.

- Chris thinks recess is ____ on rainy days. (**dull**)

- Yuki wants to ____ a vegetable garden in her backyard. (**create**)

- When I was little, I played with a soft baseball bat. Now I use a ____ bat. (**firm**)

- A ____ saves someone from danger. (**hero**)

3 Read each sentence and ask students to tell which word or words are wrong. Then have them provide the correct word from the week's list.

- That chair is as soft as a rock. (**soft/firm**)

- The bad guy saved a boy's life by driving him to the hospital. (**bad guy/hero**)

- The movie was so interesting, it put me to sleep. (**interesting/dull**)

- Molly will destroy a card to give to her mom on Mother's Day. (**destroy/create**)

4 Read each sentence and ask students to decide if it is true or false. If the sentence is false, instruct students to explain why.

- A hero is brave and good. (**true**)

- A firm object makes a good pillow. (**false; a firm object would be hard and uncomfortable for your head**)

- The word *create* means to copy someone's idea. (**false; *create* means to make something from your own ideas**)

- The word *dull* means about the same as *boring*. (**true**)

Answers for page 23: 1. B, 2. F, 3. D, 4. H

Review Words	hero • dull • create • firm

Fill in the bubble next to the correct answer.

1. Which sentence uses the word *create* correctly?
Ⓐ Please neatly create your name at the top of this page.
Ⓑ Sean decided to create a story about his pet lizard.
Ⓒ Sarah created her dog to the park every afternoon.
Ⓓ Create my hand as we walk across the street.

2. Which is *firm*?
Ⓕ the top of a table
Ⓖ raindrops
Ⓗ milk
Ⓙ a blanket

3. People called Ms. Pine a *hero* because she ___.
Ⓐ acted on television
Ⓑ painted beautiful pictures
Ⓒ wrote a funny book for children
Ⓓ rescued some hikers during a forest fire

4. A *dull* story is ___.
Ⓕ funny
Ⓖ scary
Ⓗ boring
Ⓙ interesting

Writing

Write about a hero. Use **hero** in your sentence.

_____

_____

gloomy

adjective

Someone who is **gloomy** feels sad.

Ben felt **gloomy** after his dog ran away from home.

When might you feel **gloomy**?

- when you're eating pizza
- when your cat is sick
- when you win a ballgame
- when you're going to the toy store
- when you have a cold and can't go to a birthday party

What do you do to cheer up when you feel **gloomy**?
How can you cheer up a friend who feels **gloomy**?

prefer

verb

You **prefer** something when you like it better than other things.

Annie **prefers** chocolate ice cream to vanilla.

Which of the two in each pair do you **prefer**?

- hamburgers or pizza
- make-believe stories or stories about real people
- cats or dogs
- crayons or markers
- playing outside or playing inside

Do you **prefer** apples or bananas? Why do you **prefer** that fruit?

clever

adjective

A **clever** person is smart and can quickly figure things out.

The **clever** police officer looked at the clues and figured out who had robbed the store.

Would you be **clever** if you:

- learned all of your spelling words in one day?
- decided what to eat for breakfast?
- guessed the ending to a story before anyone else?
- invented a homework machine?
- ate all your lunch at recess?

Describe something **clever** that you've done at home.
Describe something **clever** that you've done at school.

screech

noun

A **screech** is a loud, high-pitched noise that may sound scary.

When the car stopped suddenly, its brakes made a **screech**.

Which of the following might make a **screech**?

- a sleeping baby
- rocks tumbling down a hill
- snowflakes falling from the sky
- someone playing an electric guitar
- hungry parrots

Make the sound of a **screech**.
What animals might make **screeches**?
What nonliving things might make **screeches**?

gloomy • prefer • clever • screech

Write on the board the four words studied this week. Read the words with the class and briefly review their meanings. Then conduct the oral activities below.

1 Tell students that you are going to give them a clue about one of the words for the week. They are to find the word that answers the clue.

- You could use this word to describe a person who is very good at math. **(clever)**

- You might use this word if you said that you like the color green better than red. **(prefer)**

- This word describes someone who is very sad. **(gloomy)**

- An owl or a parrot might make one. **(a screech)**

2 Read each sentence and ask students to supply the correct word to complete the sentence.

- I ____ fresh tomatoes to canned ones. **(prefer)**

- Mary felt ____ because she was too sick to go to the zoo. **(gloomy)**

- The parrot made a loud ____ of fear when it saw a leopard. **(screech)**

- The ____ baker made a cake that looked like a castle. **(clever)**

3 Read each sentence and ask students to tell which word is wrong. Then have them provide the correct word from the week's list.

- Max felt cheery after his birthday party was cancelled. **(cheery/gloomy)**

- The foolish woman made a beautiful blanket from small scraps of cloth. **(foolish/clever)**

- I heard the monkey make silence as it demanded their food. **(silence/screech)**

- I dislike carrots more than celery, so I eat carrots every day. **(dislike/prefer)**

4 Read each sentence and ask students to decide if it is true or false. If the sentence is false, instruct students to explain why.

- When an airplane lands on a runway its brakes make a screech. **(true)**

- When you prefer a certain toy, you like it better than other toys. **(true)**

- A clever person makes wrong choices. **(false; a clever person makes smart choices)**

- Winning first place in a contest would make most people feel gloomy. **(false; most people would be happy to win a contest)**

Answers for page 27: 1. C, 2. H, 3. A, 4. F

| Review Words | gloomy • prefer • clever • screech |

Fill in the bubble next to the correct answer.

1. Which sentence tells about a *gloomy* person?
- Ⓐ Hallie smiled and clapped when her team won the game.
- Ⓑ Bret frowned because he did not understand the question.
- Ⓒ Uncle Mike was too sad to eat his dinner.
- Ⓓ Aunt Cathy giggled at Rose Ann's jokes.

2. What can make a *screech*?
- Ⓕ thunder during a storm
- Ⓖ water from a drinking fountain
- Ⓗ a bird in a jungle
- Ⓙ ocean waves

3. Which sentence tells about a *clever* person?
- Ⓐ Amy learned to speak Spanish during summer vacation.
- Ⓑ Alexander was the first student to walk into the classroom.
- Ⓒ Bart wears a warm jacket and gloves when it snows.
- Ⓓ Lily ate the bag of popcorn all by herself.

4. Which sentence uses the word *prefer* correctly?
- Ⓕ I prefer chocolate chip cookies to oatmeal raisin.
- Ⓖ My dog Mazy can prefer faster than your dog.
- Ⓗ Jessie and Paul prefer their toys with their friends.
- Ⓙ I need to prefer a gift to give to Molly for her birthday.

| Writing |

Write about two games. Tell which one you prefer. Use **prefer** in your sentence.

_____

_____

breeze

noun

A **breeze** is a light and gentle wind.

A cool **breeze** feels good on a hot day.

Which things can a **breeze** move?

- flowers in a garden
- a car on a highway
- a squirrel in a tree
- a small kite in the sky
- the fence around a house

Name some other things that a **breeze** could move. What are some other things that a **breeze** is not strong enough to move?

discuss

verb

People **discuss** something when they talk about it.

Let's **discuss** the best places to visit when we go on our family vacation.

What might first-graders like to **discuss**?

- favorite television shows
- the best toys
- games to play at recess
- where to go to college
- the best soap for washing clothes

What are things you **discuss** in school? What are things you like to **discuss** with a friend?

famous

adjective

A **famous** person is someone whom most people know about or recognize.

The crowd clapped and cheered when the **famous** singer rode by in the parade.

Which actions could make a person **famous**?

- inventing the first computer
- baking yummy cookies for family members
- being the best baseball player on the best team
- playing the piano too loudly
- starring in a big movie

Pretend you are a **famous** person. Tell why you are **famous**.

glance

verb

When you **glance** at something, you look quickly at it.

Before we leave for school, Mom **glances** at me to see if my hair is combed.

Why might you **glance** at something?

- to see if your shoelaces are tied
- to read a story
- to watch a parade
- to see if your teacher is in the classroom
- to see if it's raining

Show what you do when you **glance** out the window.
Who or what might you **glance** at in school?
Tell about times in school when you might need to take longer looks rather than just **glancing**.

breeze • discuss • famous • glance

Write on the board the four words studied this week. Read the words with the class and briefly review their meanings. Then conduct the oral activities below.

1 Tell students that you are going to give them a clue about one of the words for the week. They are to find the word that answers the clue.

- Your class might do this after reading a story. (**discuss it**)

- You do this when you look quickly at something. (**glance at it**)

- This word describes Dr. Seuss, the man who wrote and illustrated *Green Eggs and Ham*. (**famous**)

- This kind of wind can move the leaves on a tree. (**a breeze**)

2 Read each sentence and ask students to supply the correct word to complete the sentence.

- The president of the United States is a very ____ person. (**famous**)

- A ____ pushed my toy sailboat across the pond. (**breeze**)

- After we visit the zoo, we will ____ the animals we saw. (**discuss**)

- Before I start the car, I ____ to make sure that my children have buckled their seat belts. (**glance**)

3 Read each sentence and ask students to tell which word or words are wrong. Then have them provide the correct word from the week's list.

- The tornado gently moved the flowers back and forth. (**tornado/breeze**)

- Everyone took pictures of the unknown movie star as she got out of the limousine. (**unknown/famous**)

- Mom asked me to stare out the window to see if the newspaper was on the porch. (**stare/glance**)

- Soon it will be your birthday! Let's not talk about the kind of party you want to have. (**not talk about/discuss**)

4 Read each sentence and ask students to decide if it is true or false. If the sentence is false, instruct students to explain why.

- A famous TV star is a person whom no one has heard of. (**false; a famous TV star is someone whom many people recognize**)

- When you glance at the clock, you take a quick look. (**true**)

- To *discuss* means to listen carefully to all the sounds you can hear. (**false; to** *discuss* **means to talk about something with someone**)

- A breeze can knock over a tree. (**false; a breeze is a light wind that is not strong enough to knock over a tree**)

Answers for page 31: 1. A, 2. G, 3. B, 4. H

| **Review Words** | breeze • discuss • famous • glance |

Fill in the bubble next to the correct answer.

1. When you *glance* at someone, you ___.
- Ⓐ take a quick look
- Ⓑ close your eyes
- Ⓒ listen carefully
- Ⓓ stare for a long time

2. A *breeze* is a gentle ___.
- Ⓕ touch
- Ⓖ wind
- Ⓗ voice
- Ⓙ animal

3. When you *discuss* your ideas, you ___.
- Ⓐ never tell anyone about them
- Ⓑ talk about them with someone
- Ⓒ write them down
- Ⓓ read about them

4. Which sentence tells about a *famous* person?
- Ⓕ Aunt Rosemary trained her dog to roll over.
- Ⓖ Meg is the fastest swimmer at our school.
- Ⓗ Neil Armstrong was the first person to walk on the moon.
- Ⓙ Jeff Blackwood grilled the best hamburgers I ever ate.

Writing

Write about a famous person. Use **famous** in your sentence.

_____

_____

entrance

noun

The **entrance** is the way into a place.

A car blocked the **entrance** to the school parking lot.

Which things need an **entrance**?

- an egg
- a house
- a supermarket
- a kitchen table
- a restaurant

Describe the **entrance** to your school. Describe the **entrance** to your home.

chatter

verb

When you **chatter**, you talk about things that are not important.

Dad and his friends often **chatter** about the kinds of cars they like.

Which people are **chattering**?

- Pepita and Carrie are talking about shoes.
- Your mom and your teacher are talking about how you are doing in school.
- Your dad and his doctor are talking about the medicine your dad needs to take.
- Charlie and Hank are talking about their favorite football teams.
- The president of the United States is making a speech on television.

What do you like to **chatter** about with your friends?

popular

adjective

If a thing is **popular**, many people like it.

Dogs and cats are **popular** pets in many places around the world.

Which are **popular** sports?

- football
- racing goats
- baseball
- basketball
- rolling cheese down a hill

Tell the name of a game you like to play. Do you think that game is **popular**? Count how many other students in the class like to play that game, too.

scrub

verb

To **scrub** something, you rub it very hard to clean it.

I will have to **scrub** that pot because there is burned food stuck inside it.

Which need to be **scrubbed**?

- a floor with sticky peanut butter on it
- muddy hands and fingernails
- a baby with food on her face
- the dirt left behind in a bathtub
- a dusty table

Show what you do when you **scrub** something. What are some good **scrubbing** tools?

entrance • chatter • popular • scrub

Write on the board the four words studied this week. Read the words with the class and briefly review their meanings. Then conduct the oral activities below.

1 Tell students that you are going to give them a clue about one of the words for the week. They are to find the word that answers the clue.

- You should do this to an icky, sticky floor. **(scrub it)**

- This word describes a person who has many friends. **(popular)**

- Many kids do this before the school bell rings in the morning. **(chatter)**

- Every house needs one of these. **(an entrance)**

2 Read each sentence and ask students to supply the correct word to complete the sentence.

- During recess , some older students like to ____ instead of playing games. **(chatter)**

- Dan planted flowers in the garden, so now he needs to ____ his hands. **(scrub)**

- The ____ to our house is a large red door. **(entrance)**

- Birds are ____ pets in most countries. **(popular)**

3 Read each sentence and ask students to tell which word is wrong. Then have them provide the correct word from the week's list.

- Tony is unknown because he is the best player on the soccer team. **(unknown/popular)**

- Most guests use the exit to come into our home. **(exit/entrance)**

- Dad will have to dry the dirty grill to get it clean. **(dry/scrub)**

4 Read each sentence and ask students to decide if it is true or false. If the sentence is false, instruct students to explain why.

- The entrance to a building is usually a door. **(true)**

- Popular people can get many party invitations. **(true)**

- You work hard when you scrub something clean. **(true)**

- When people chatter, they talk about important things. **(false; when people chatter, they discuss unimportant things)**

Answers for page 35: 1. D, 2. F, 3. A, 4. G

Review Words	entrance • chatter • popular • scrub

Fill in the bubble next to the correct answer.

1. Which sentence uses the word *entrance* correctly?
- Ⓐ She left an entrance in her backpack.
- Ⓑ The entrance has a sign that says "EXIT."
- Ⓒ Our principal likes to entrance with a smile.
- Ⓓ The entrance to the cave is dark.

2. If you *chatter*, you ____.
- Ⓕ talk about things that don't matter
- Ⓖ talk about very important things
- Ⓗ listen to the news on the radio
- Ⓙ shout as loudly as you can

3. You might *scrub* your feet if they were very ____.
- Ⓐ dirty
- Ⓑ pretty
- Ⓒ clean
- Ⓓ sore

4. Which sentence uses the word *popular* correctly?
- Ⓕ They like to popular while they jog around the track.
- Ⓖ Soccer is a popular sport for kids to play.
- Ⓗ The popular stands tall outside my bedroom window.
- Ⓙ Greg is so popular that no one knows him.

Writing

Write about the entrance to a special place. Use **entrance** in your sentence.

_____

_____

pest

noun

A **pest** is someone or something that really bothers you.

Ants can be **pests** when they walk all over our picnic food.

Which are **pests**?

- a friend who shares toys with you
- someone who shows you how to add numbers
- mosquitoes that buzz when you're trying to sleep
- someone who won't stop teasing you
- flies that land on your food

Name someone or something you think is a **pest**.
What is a good way to handle that **pest**? Do you ever act like a **pest**?

boast

verb

When you **boast**, you talk with too much pride about yourself.

We were tired of hearing Casey **boast** about the home run he hit.

Which of these speakers are **boasting**?

- "I can spell better than anyone!"
- "My mom bought me a new backpack."
- "Do you need some help?"
- "My dad's car cost a lot more than your dad's car."
- "My house has twelve rooms and a swimming pool."

How do you feel when you hear someone **boast**?
Tell something good about yourself without **boasting**.

scamper

verb

Something **scampers** when it runs quickly and lightly.

My cat watches squirrels **scamper** up and down an oak tree.

Which animals can **scamper**?

- an elephant
- a moth
- a mouse
- a rabbit
- a fox

What are some reasons why an animal might **scamper**? Can a person **scamper**? If so, **scamper** around the classroom.

strange

adjective

Something that is **strange** is odd or unusual.

We all stared at the **strange** sight of a man walking down the street on his hands.

Which of these would be a **strange** sight to see?

- a car in a tree
- a girl riding a bicycle
- the sun in the daytime
- a talking fish
- a man as tall as a building

What sights would be **strange** to see on the playground? What sights would be **strange** to see in your home?

pest • boast • scamper • strange

Write on the board the four words studied this week. Read the words with the class and briefly review their meanings. Then conduct the oral activities below.

1 Tell students that you are going to give them a clue about one of the words for the week. They are to find the word that answers the clue.

- This word could describe a cat that has six toes on one paw. **(strange)**

- You might call a mosquito this. **(a pest)**

- Mice do this to get away from cats. **(scamper)**

- People do this if they tell you over and over about their accomplishments. **(boast)**

2 Read each sentence and ask students to supply the correct word to complete the sentence.

- Crissy likes to ____ about all the clothes she has. **(boast)**

- My brother is such a ____ when he pulls my ponytail! **(pest)**

- As soon as they hear me pick up the bag of cat food, my cats ____ into the room. **(scamper)**

- The ____ shadows on the wall scared me. **(strange)**

3 Read each sentence and ask students to tell which word or words are wrong. Then have them provide the correct word from the week's list.

- The squirrels slide up the tree when my dog chases them. **(slide/scamper)**

- A snake with two heads is an ordinary animal. **(an ordinary/a strange)**

- A fly is a helpful bug that carries germs. **(helpful bug/pest)**

- Stacey likes to show off her trophy and keep quiet about her team. **(keep quiet/boast)**

4 Read each sentence and ask students to decide if it is true or false. If the sentence is false, instruct students to explain why.

- Whales scamper through ocean waves. **(false; whales don't run, they swim)**

- To some people, eating octopus seems like a strange thing to do. **(true)**

- *Boast* and *brag* have about the same meaning. **(true)**

- Cows are pests because they give us milk and cheese. **(false; cows provide food, so they are helpful animals, not pests)**

Answers for page 39: 1. B, 2. H, 3. A, 4. H

| **Review Words** | pest • boast • scamper • strange |

Fill in the bubble next to the correct answer.

1. Which sentence uses the word _boast_ correctly?

Ⓐ Dad will boast to the plumber that the pipes need fixing.

Ⓑ Matt likes to boast that he is the strongest boy in class.

Ⓒ Gemma needs to boast so that she can win the drawing contest.

Ⓓ Let's boast a song about our school.

2. Which sentence tells about a _pest_?

Ⓕ James reads a story to his little sister every night.

Ⓖ Camels carry people across hot deserts.

Ⓗ A gopher ate the flowers in my garden.

Ⓙ Ana lets her sister wear her clothes.

3. Which animal can _scamper_?

Ⓐ a rabbit

Ⓑ a hippo

Ⓒ an owl

Ⓓ a goldfish

4. Which sentence tells about something _strange_?

Ⓕ Lee plays in the sand at the beach.

Ⓖ Robins are birds that eat worms.

Ⓗ Butterflies taste food with their feet.

Ⓙ Kate skates on ice.

| **Writing** |

Write about someone who acts like a pest. Use **pest** in your sentence.

_____

_____

wiggle

verb

You **wiggle** when you twist and turn from side to side in a jerky way.

It's fun to **wiggle** when you dance.

Which can you **wiggle**?

- your tongue
- your hair
- your nose
- your knees
- your fingers

Show what you do when you **wiggle** your body. What can you do about a tooth that **wiggles**?

bashful

adjective

Someone who is **bashful** feels shy, especially around new people.

The new student was so **bashful** that she looked down when the teacher introduced her.

When might you feel **bashful**?

- when you talk to your dog
- when you play with your best friend
- when you meet the president of the United States
- when you read a poem in front of the whole school
- when you're new to a group and have to speak

Have you ever felt **bashful**? Why did you feel **bashful**?

harbor

noun

A **harbor** is a place next to the land where ships and boats are kept.

The ship sailed into the **harbor**, where it would be safe from the storm.

Which of these do people keep in a **harbor**?

- farm animals
- sailboats
- buses
- airplanes
- ships

Is a **harbor** on land or in the water?
What kinds of animals might live in a **harbor**?

soar

verb

Birds and planes **soar** when they glide or fly high in the sky.

Eagles sometimes **soar** through the air without flapping their wings.

Which can **soar** through the air?

- hawks
- airplanes
- chickens
- penguins
- kites

Show how you would **soar** through the air if you were a bird.
If you have been on a plane, tell what it was like to **soar** above the clouds.

wiggle • bashful • harbor • soar

Write on the board the four words studied this week. Read the words with the class and briefly review their meanings. Then conduct the oral activities below.

1 Tell students that you are going to give them a clue about one of the words for the week. They are to find the word that answers the clue.

- Worms do this if you touch them. **(wiggle)**

- This word names a place where boats and ships are parked. **(harbor)**

- Sea gulls do this when they fly. **(soar)**

- This word describes someone who feels shy. **(bashful)**

2 Read each sentence and ask students to supply the correct word to complete the sentence.

- Airplanes are kept in an airport, and ships are kept in a _____. **(harbor)**

- Hawks _____ high in the sky, searching for mice on the ground. **(soar)**

- I sometimes feel _____ when I meet a friend's parents. **(bashful)**

- I saw a little snake _____ through the grass. **(wiggle)**

3 Read each sentence and ask students to tell which word or words are wrong. Then have them provide the correct word from the week's list.

- It's fun to watch a kite crash in the air. **(crash/soar)**

- I can make the pudding stay still when I move the bowl back and forth. **(stay still/wiggle)**

- Billy was so brave when he met the astronaut that he looked down and whispered hello. **(brave/bashful)**

- Ships and boats are kept safe in a bus station. **(bus station/harbor)**

4 Read each sentence and ask students to decide if it is true or false. If the sentence is false, instruct students to explain why.

- A bashful person finds it easy to meet new people. **(false; a bashful person is shy, especially when meeting someone new)**

- An airplane soars as it lands on a runway. **(false; an airplane soars when it flies high in the sky)**

- Puppies often wiggle if you pick them up. **(true)**

- A harbor needs to have deep water so ships can sail into it without getting stuck. **(true)**

Answers for page 43: 1. C, 2. F, 3. B, 4. J

| Review Words | wiggle • bashful • harbor • soar |

Fill in the bubble next to the correct answer.

1. Which are kept in a *harbor*?

Ⓐ ships and airplanes
Ⓑ cars and buses
Ⓒ boats and ships
Ⓓ scooters and bicycles

2. Which sentence tells about a *bashful* person?

Ⓕ Brad turned red when he met his new teacher.
Ⓖ Nathan walked up to the new student and said hi.
Ⓗ Kim smiled and welcomed each visitor to the school.
Ⓙ Jeff sang at the party for new students and their families.

3. Which animals *wiggle* when they move?

Ⓐ butterflies
Ⓑ snakes
Ⓒ eagles
Ⓓ ladybugs

4. When you *soar,* you are ____.

Ⓕ in a hole
Ⓖ on a hill
Ⓗ in the ocean
Ⓙ in the sky

Writing

Write about something that makes you wiggle. Use **wiggle** in your sentence.

_____

_____

jabber

verb

When you **jabber**, you talk fast and make little sense.

When Ryan gets excited, he often **jabbers** so fast that we can't understand him.

When might you **jabber**?

- when you have a new idea to share
- when you are sleepy and yawning
- when you want to tell about your new bike
- when you have nothing to say
- when you tell your name

Have you ever heard someone **jabber**?
Show how you might **jabber** if you were excited or scared.

damp

adjective

A **damp** object is a little bit wet.

My dog does not like baths, so I use a **damp** towel to clean her.

If you left your jacket outside, which might make it **damp**?

- sunshine
- a breeze
- a heavy rainstorm
- a foggy night
- a light drizzle of rain

Have you ever felt anything that was **damp**? What was it?
Why was it **damp**?

task

noun

A **task** is a small job or chore.

My sister's **task** is to set the table for dinner.

Which of the following are **tasks**?

- washing the car
- watching a movie
- mowing the lawn
- playing basketball
- emptying the dishwasher

Tell about the **tasks** you do at home. How often do you do them? Which is your favorite **task**? Which is your least favorite **task**?

dismiss

verb

When you **dismiss** people, you let them leave.

Mr. Powell will **dismiss** us from school when the bell rings.

Which mean about the same as **dismiss**?

- to send people home
- to welcome people
- to let people leave
- to send people away
- to let people come inside

How does your teacher **dismiss** you from the classroom? Show how you would **dismiss** the class if you were the teacher.

---

jabber • damp • task • dismiss

Write on the board the four words studied this week. Read the words with the class and briefly review their meanings. Then conduct the oral activities below.

1 Tell students that you are going to give them a clue about one of the words for the week. They are to find the word that answers the clue.

- This word describes a towel that is just a little wet. **(damp)**

- Teachers do this to their students at the end of the school day. **(dismiss them)**

- You might do this if you were talking in a very excited. **(jabber)**

- This word describes a chore such as dusting the furniture. **(a task)**

2 Read each sentence and ask students to supply the correct word to complete the sentence.

- Our teacher will ____ us when we have all finished the test. **(dismiss)**

- My ____ in school is to empty the pencil sharpener. **(task)**

- Little children often ____ when they are learning how to talk. **(jabber)**

- My brother uses a ____ rag to clean the mud off his soccer shoes. **(damp)**

3 Read each sentence and ask students to tell which word or words are wrong. Then have them provide the correct word from the week's list.

- Cleaning my room is not my favorite game. **(game/task)**

- My best friend and I like to be silent on the phone. **(be silent/jabber)**

- Dad put a load of dry clothes into the dryer. **(dry/damp)**

- Each day, our teacher welcomes us at two o'clock in the afternoon. **(welcomes/dismisses)**

4 Read each sentence and ask students to decide if it is true or false. If the sentence is false, instruct students to explain why.

- *Jabber* means about the same as *chatter*. **(true)**

- Drops of water fall from a damp towel. **(false; a damp towel is not wet enough to drip)**

- Sleeping and breathing are tasks. **(false; they are not jobs or chores; your body does them to stay alive)**

- To dismiss means to send away. **(true)**

Answers for page 47: 1. B, 2. J, 3. A, 4. H

Review Words	jabber • damp • task • dismiss

Fill in the bubble next to the correct answer.

1. Which word has about the same meaning as *task*?

Ⓒ game

Ⓑ job

Ⓔ idea

Ⓕ party

2. What might your teacher say when it is time to *dismiss* the class?

Ⓓ "I am happy to see you again."

Ⓖ "Please come in."

Ⓗ "Welcome!"

Ⓚ "It's time to go home. Good-bye."

3. Which sentence uses the word *jabber* correctly?

Ⓒ My big brother seems to jabber on the phone all day long.

Ⓑ Shayna can jabber her math homework faster than Mazy.

Ⓔ Be sure to use a sharp pencil to jabber your answers.

Ⓕ It is not nice to jabber someone with your elbow.

4. Which could make you *damp*?

Ⓓ swimming in a pool

Ⓖ taking a shower

Ⓗ walking in a light rain

Ⓚ sitting in the sun

Writing

Write about a task you do at home. Use **task** in your sentence.

_____

_____

busybody

noun

A **busybody** is nosy and wants to know everyone else's business.

Ana is a **busybody** who stands close to me and tries to hear everything I say to my friend.

Which might a **busybody** do?

- ask a lot of personal questions
- listen to other people's conversations
- talk about favorite toys
- take turns playing a game
- try to learn other people's secrets

Is it polite to be a **busybody**?
Is every person who asks questions a **busybody**?
What kind of things might a **busybody** want to know?

fetch

verb

When you **fetch**, you go and get something.

My mom asked me to **fetch** her car keys from the kitchen table.

Which of these might a dog learn to **fetch**?

- a stick
- a computer
- a ball
- a newspaper
- a chair

What are some things that your teacher asks students to **fetch**? Have you ever seen a dog **fetch**? What did the dog **fetch**?

regret

verb

You **regret** something when you are sorry about it.

I **regret** calling my friend a name that made him cry.

Which actions might you **regret**?

- telling a secret that someone asked you to keep
- getting all the words right on your spelling test
- giving someone a birthday present
- breaking a pair of glasses by accident
- teasing your brother

What is one thing you **regret** doing? Why do you **regret** what you did?

splendid

adjective

Something that is **splendid** is beautiful or magnificent.

The **splendid** sunset splashed the sky with pink, orange, and purple streaks.

Which are ways to describe something **splendid**?

- Wonderful!
- Fabulous!
- Icky!
- Super!
- Boring!

What **splendid** sights have you seen? Explain why you think they looked **splendid**.

busybody • fetch • regret • splendid

Write on the board the four words studied this week. Read the words with the class and briefly review their meanings. Then conduct the oral activities below.

1 Tell students that you are going to give them a clue about one of the words for the week. They are to find the word that answers the clue.

- You could use this word to describe a beautiful waterfall tumbling down a cliff. (**splendid**)

- This person wants to know everything about everybody. (**a busybody**)

- You might do this after making a bad choice. (**regret it**)

- If you throw a ball for a dog, the dog might do this. (**fetch**)

2 Read each sentence and ask students to supply the correct word to complete the sentence.

- The castle we visited was huge and ____. (**splendid**)

- Please ____ my coat from the hall closet. (**fetch**)

- I'm sorry. I ____ that I laughed at you. (**regret**)

- A ____ wants to know what everyone is doing. (**busybody**)

3 Read each sentence and ask students to tell which word or words are wrong. Then have them provide the correct word from the week's list.

- The coach asked me to lose the bats and balls for the game. (**lose/fetch**)

- Most people think the Grand Canyon is boring. (**boring/splendid**)

- I am glad that I missed the circus when I had the measles. (**am glad/regret**)

4 Read each sentence and ask students to decide if it is true or false. If the sentence is false, instruct students to explain why.

- A busybody might listen to your private phone conversations. (**true**)

- To fetch means to go and get something. (**true**)

- You can use the word *splendid* to describe a dirty old dress. (**false; something splendid is beautiful**)

- The word *regret* means *to be sorry about*. (**true**)

Answers for page 51: 1. C, 2. J, 3. B, 4. G

Review Words	busybody • fetch • regret • splendid

Fill in the bubble next to the correct answer.

1. When you *regret* doing something, you ___.
- Ⓐ are happy you did it
- Ⓑ want to do it
- Ⓒ are sorry you did it
- Ⓓ say that you will do it again

2. When you *fetch* your coat, you ___.
- Ⓕ leave your coat where it is
- Ⓖ get a new coat
- Ⓗ lose your coat
- Ⓙ go and get your coat

3. Which is something *splendid*?
- Ⓐ litter lying by the side of a road
- Ⓑ a double rainbow in the sky
- Ⓒ a toy car
- Ⓓ an oil spill in the ocean

4. Which sentence tells about a *busybody*?
- Ⓕ Mom asks me about my day when I get home from school.
- Ⓖ Tyler wants to know everything that goes on in my family.
- Ⓗ Dad asks me what's wrong when I seem sad.
- Ⓙ When Charlie calls, he always asks, "What's up?"

Writing

Write about a pretend thing that is splendid. Use **splendid** in your sentence.

_____

_____

snoop

verb

You **snoop** when you sneak a look at something.

I **snooped** under Mom and Dad's bed to see if my birthday presents were hidden there.

Who was **snooping**?

- Adam watched his neighbors through a hole in the fence.
- The dentist looked inside my mouth to check my teeth.
- Ruby read her sister's diary without asking.
- Mandy smiled as she watched the baby sleep.
- Martin looked out the window to watch the sun set.

Pretend you are as small as a bug and can climb walls like one. Where would you **snoop**? What would you want to find out?

texture

noun

Texture is the way something feels or looks.

A baby's skin has a soft, smooth **texture** like rose petals.

Which words describe **textures**?

- rough
- fluffy
- sweet
- silky
- sticky
- bumpy

What are the **textures** of the clothes you're wearing? What are some **textures** that you see and feel in the classroom?

wavy

adjective

A **wavy** line has curves and is not straight.

My skirt has **wavy** lines that go up and down like ocean waves.

Which could be **wavy**?

- a roller coaster track
- seaweed
- hair
- a soccer ball
- lightning

Use your hand to make **wavy** lines in the air.
Are there things in the classroom that are **wavy**?
What are they?

grouchy

adjective

A **grouchy** person is in a bad mood.

My little brother is **grouchy** when he doesn't get enough sleep.

Which of these would make you **grouchy**?

- having to walk your dog while your favorite TV show is on
- getting presents for your birthday
- forgetting to bring your lunch to school
- seeing your best work hanging on the classroom wall
- losing your homework

What is something that makes you **grouchy**?
Who or what helps you get out of a **grouchy** mood?

snoop • texture • wavy • grouchy

Write on the board the four words studied this week. Read the words with the class and briefly review their meanings. Then conduct the oral activities below.

1 Tell students that you are going to give them a clue about one of the words for the week. They are to find the word that answers the clue.

- Words like *rough* and *slimy* describe this. (**texture**)

- A person who is in a bad mood feels this way. (**grouchy**)

- A sneaky person might do this. (**snoop**)

- This word describes a line that is squiggly or curvy. (**wavy**)

2 Read each sentence and ask students to supply the correct word to complete the sentence.

- My hair is straight, but my dad's hair is ____. (**wavy**)

- My little brother likes to ____ through my older brother's closet. (**snoop**)

- My baby sister gets ____ if she doesn't take her nap. (**grouchy**)

- My favorite stuffed animal is a lamb that has a fluffy ____. (**texture**)

3 Read each sentence and ask students to tell which word is wrong. Then have them provide the correct word from the week's list.

- I am cheery when I don't get enough sleep. (**cheery/grouchy**)

- A frog's skin has a smooth, slippery odor. (**odor/texture**)

- I drew a straight line to show how a kangaroo goes up and down as it hops. (**straight/wavy**)

4 Read each sentence and ask students to decide if it is true or false. If the sentence is false, instruct students to explain why.

- A busybody might snoop in order to learn people's secrets. (**true**)

- You can use a ruler to make a wavy line. (**false; you use a ruler to make straight lines; a wavy line is not straight**)

- Sour is a texture. (**false; sour is the way something tastes**)

- People are grouchy when they are happy. (**false; people are grouchy when they are in a bad mood**)

Answers for page 55: 1. B, 2. J, 3. C, 4. G

Name _____

Fill in the bubble next to the correct answer.

1. Which is true about *texture*?

Ⓐ Textures are sounds that you hear.

Ⓑ Everything you can touch has a texture.

Ⓒ All textures feel smooth and slippery.

Ⓓ All textures feel rough and bumpy.

2. What does it mean to *snoop*?

Ⓕ to laugh out loud at a joke

Ⓖ to whisper a secret to someone

Ⓗ to play outside in the sunshine

Ⓙ to sneak a peek at something

3. When something is *wavy*, it ___.

Ⓐ is round like a circle

Ⓑ is straight

Ⓒ has curves

Ⓓ is shaped like a square

4. Which sentence tells about someone who is *grouchy*?

Ⓕ Maria cheered when she made the basket that won the game.

Ⓖ James mumbled and threw his catcher's mitt on the ground.

Ⓗ Phillip raised his hand to ask his teacher a question.

Ⓙ Sheena held her teddy bear as she slept.

Writing

Write about something that has a texture you like. Use **texture** in your sentence.

_____

_____

handy

adjective

Something that is **handy** is useful.

A backpack is a **handy** bag for carrying things to school.

Which are **handy** things to have in a classroom?

- bookshelves
- a pencil sharpener
- a garden hose
- computers
- a camping tent

What is something you think is **handy**? How do you use that **handy** thing?

dine

verb

When you **dine**, you eat dinner.

My family usually **dines** at our kitchen table around six o'clock at night.

Which of the following are times to **dine**?

- 7:00 a.m.
- 5:00 p.m.
- 6:30 p.m.
- noon
- 2:00 p.m.

At what time do you usually **dine**? Where do you **dine** at your house? Do you ever **dine** out? Where do you **dine** out?

present

verb

To **present** means to show or introduce something.

The circus ringmaster called out to the crowd, "I now **present** the Great Bandini!"

Which could you **present** during show-and-tell at school?

- a real elephant
- a small car that you made out of wood
- flowers from your garden
- a trophy you won
- a tree that grows in your yard

Who is someone you would like to **present** to your teacher? Name some things that you might want to **present** to your class.

poky

adjective

Someone or something that moves slowly is **poky**.

Sometimes my dog is **poky** on walks because she stops to smell everything she sees.

Which of the following are **poky**?

- a snail crossing a sidewalk
- a runner who is winning a race
- a turtle crawling in the grass
- a lion chasing a zebra
- a sleepy child getting dressed for school

Name some people and animals that are **poky**. When are you **poky**? Show how you walk when you are **poky**.

handy • dine • present • poky

Write on the board the four words studied this week. Read the words with the class and briefly review their meanings. Then conduct the oral activities below.

❶ Tell students that you are going to give them a clue about one of the words for the week. They are to find the word that answers the clue.

- You do this when you introduce two people. **(present them to each other)**

- This word might describe a snail or a tortoise. **(poky)**

- This word describes useful kitchen tools. **(handy)**

- This is what people do at the evening meal. **(dine)**

❷ Read each sentence and ask students to supply the correct word to complete the sentence.

- The _____ lady took her time answering the doorbell. **(poky)**

- My mom and dad are going to _____ at a fancy restaurant tonight. **(dine)**

- I like to read before I go to sleep, so it's _____ to have a lamp next to my bed. **(handy)**

- My sister's high school is going to _____ a play called *Our Town*. **(present)**

❸ Read each sentence and ask students to tell which word is wrong. Then have them provide the correct word from the week's list.

- Every Sunday evening, my grandparents join us as we sleep at our dining room table. **(sleep/dine)**

- Our principal will hide our guest, a police officer who will speak to us about safety. **(hide/present)**

- My grandpa seems speedy because he is never in a hurry. **(speedy/poky)**

- A flashlight is a useless thing to have when the lights go out. **(useless/handy)**

❹ Read each sentence and ask students to decide if it is true or false. If the sentence is false, instruct students to explain why.

- *Handy* means about the same as *useful*. **(true)**

- "May I present my friend Matty?" means "May I introduce my friend Matty?" **(true)**

- A good time to dine is before you go to school in the morning. **(false; when you dine, you eat dinner)**

- It is important to be poky when there is a fire drill. **(false; you should move quickly during a fire drill)**

Answers for page 59: 1. D, 2. H, 3. A, 4. G

Review Words   handy • dine • present • poky

Fill in the bubble next to the correct answer.

1. **When is a good time to be *poky*?**
   Ⓐ when you are running a race
   Ⓑ when your dad asks you to hurry
   Ⓒ when you are already late for school
   Ⓓ when you look at interesting things in a museum

2. **Which sentence uses the word *present* correctly?**
   Ⓕ Please present your oatmeal before it gets cold.
   Ⓖ My dog likes to present its paws all over the couch.
   Ⓗ "Grandpa, may I present my teacher, Ms. Wintergreen?"
   Ⓙ Please present your toys away in the closet.

3. **When do you *dine*?**
   Ⓐ in the evening
   Ⓑ at noon
   Ⓒ in the morning
   Ⓓ at snack time

4. **Which is *handy*?**
   Ⓕ a pencil without an eraser
   Ⓖ a classroom bookshelf
   Ⓗ a broken hammer
   Ⓙ a jacket pocket with a hole in it

Writing

Write about a handy thing that you keep in your room. Use **handy** in your sentence.

_____

_____

compete

verb

People who **compete** take part in contests, sports, or games.

I am going to **compete** in a spelling bee to win a big trophy.

When are you **competing**?

- when you play on a basketball team
- when you cheer for a baseball team
- when you play checkers against your mom
- when you draw a beautiful picture
- when you enter a drawing contest

In what kinds of games, sports, or contests have you **competed**? Do you like to **compete**? Why or why not?

cluttered

adjective

A **cluttered** place is messy and full of things.

The drawer is so **cluttered** that I can't find a pencil.

Which words describe **cluttered** places?

- clothes stuffed into a closet
- toys scattered all over a floor
- books standing side by side on a shelf
- a garage that has no room for a car because it is crammed full of boxes and furniture
- papers kept in folders in a desk drawer

Tell about a **cluttered** place that you have seen.
How do you keep your bedroom from getting **cluttered**?

victory

noun

When you win, you gain a **victory**.

The soccer players yelled "**Victory**!" after their team won the championship game.

Which words mean about the same as **victory**?

- a win
- a loss
- a tie
- failure
- success

Tell about a time when you won a **victory**. Show what you would do if your team had just won a **victory**.

frisky

adjective

A **frisky** animal or person is playful and lively.

The **frisky** puppy dashed wildly around the yard in circles.

Which words describe a **frisky** person or animal?

- active
- tired
- poky
- fun-loving
- full of energy

Where have you seen a **frisky** animal? What was the **frisky** animal doing?
Show what you would do if you felt **frisky**.

compete • cluttered • victory • frisky

Write on the board the four words studied this week. Read the words with the class and briefly review their meanings. Then conduct the oral activities below.

1 Tell students that you are going to give them a clue about one of the words for the week. They are to find the word that answers the clue.

- Teams do this when they play other other teams. (**compete**)

- This is what you hope for when you compete in a sport. (**a victory**)

- This word describes a messy desk that is covered with stuff. (**cluttered**)

- This word describes a playful kitten that is full of energy. (**frisky**)

2 Read each sentence and ask students to supply the correct word to complete the sentence.

- Mark's team won a 5-to-2 ____ over the Hornets. (**victory**)

- The ____ puppy tried to catch every bug it saw in the garden. (**frisky**)

- The students in my class will ____ for prizes in a writing contest. (**compete**)

- My closet is so ____ with toys and clothes that Mom says we should give some away. (**cluttered**)

3 Read each sentence and ask students to tell which word or words are wrong. Then have them provide the correct word from the week's list.

- I can't find my folder because my backpack is empty. (**empty/cluttered**)

- Taylor is a great soccer player who loves to sit on the bench. (**sit on the bench/compete**)

- Our sleepy puppy chewed two shoes and five socks while we were at the store. (**sleepy/frisky**)

- The team that scores the most points will declare a loss. (**loss/victory**)

4 Read each sentence and ask students to decide if it is true or false. If the sentence is false, instruct students to explain why.

- A cluttered room is neat and tidy. (**false; a cluttered room is messy**)

- A frisky pet likes to sleep most of the time. (**false; a frisky pet is active and playful**)

- When you win a contest, you win a victory. (**true**)

- Someone who competes a lot probably likes to play sports and games. (**true**)

Answers for page 63: 1. B, 2. J, 3. C, 4. H

| Review Words | compete • cluttered • victory • frisky |

Fill in the bubble next to the correct answer.

1. Which sentence tells about a *frisky* animal?
Ⓐ Cal's cat Cleo likes to nap in the sunshine.
Ⓑ Sparky chases everything. He even chases his own tail.
Ⓒ Fudge the puppy snores when she sleeps.
Ⓓ Brownie is a small dog who wears a sweater on cold days.

2. When you *compete,* you ___.
Ⓕ win a game
Ⓖ play by yourself
Ⓗ lose a contest
Ⓙ play against others

3. A *cluttered* room ___.
Ⓐ has very few things in it
Ⓑ is neat and tidy
Ⓒ is filled with a mess
Ⓓ has nothing in it

4. Which score shows that the Cubs won *victory* over the Tigers?
Ⓕ Tigers 6   Cubs 4
Ⓖ Tigers 2   Cubs 0
Ⓗ Tigers 4   Cubs 6
Ⓙ Tigers 3   Cubs 1

| Writing |

Write about a frisky animal. Use **frisky** in your sentence.

_____

_____

hush

verb

When you **hush**, you become quiet.

Our teacher asked everyone to **hush** so she could read us a story.

Which are times to **hush**?

- when your mom is putting the baby to sleep
- when you are meeting someone new
- when you are watching a movie in a theater
- when you answer the phone
- when you are trying to hear a faraway sound

Make a sound that means **hush**.
Use your finger to make a signal that means **hush**.

daring

adjective

A **daring** person is brave and tries adventuresome things.

My **daring** brother learned how to skydive.

Which people need to be **daring** because of the work they do?

- a pet-shop owner
- a firefighter
- an astronaut
- an author who writes books for children
- a lifeguard

Who is a **daring** person you know or have heard about?
What **daring** thing did that person do?

speck

noun

A **speck** is a small spot or a small mark.

You can hardly see it, but there is a **speck** of red ink on my white shirt.

Which words describe a **speck**?

- a puddle of spilled milk
- an eraser
- a bit of dust
- a tiny dot of paint
- a bread crumb

Look around the classroom. What **specks** do you see? Make a **speck** on the chalkboard.

tour

noun

When you go somewhere interesting, you can take a **tour** of that place to learn more about it.

My family took a **tour** of a movie studio to see how movies are made.

What should you do when you are on a museum **tour**?

- listen to the guide
- learn new information
- ask questions
- go off on your own
- stay on the bus

Have you ever taken a **tour**? What place did you visit on your **tour**? Where else would you like to take a **tour**? Show how you would guide a group of visitors who came to take a **tour** of your classroom.

hush • daring • speck • tour

Write on the board the four words studied this week. Read the words with the class and briefly review their meanings. Then conduct the oral activities below.

1 Tell students that you are going to give them a clue about one of the words for the week. They are to find the word that answers the clue.

- This is a small mark or spot. (**a speck**)

- You could use this word to describe someone who skis down steep hills. (**daring**)

- People do this when a play begins. (**hush**)

- People might take one while they are on vacation in a new place. (**a tour**)

2 Read each sentence and ask students to supply the correct word to complete the sentence.

- My ____ sister sang on stage in front of a large crowd. (**daring**)

- A flea is a bug that's as small as a ____. (**speck**)

- The students took a ____ of the White House and saw the president's office. (**tour**)

- Our teacher expects us to ____ when she begins speaking. (**hush**)

3 Read each sentence and ask students to tell which word or words are wrong. Then have them provide the correct word from the week's list.

- Be sure to talk loudly when the movie starts. (**talk loudly/hush**)

- The scared puppy walked fearlessly up to the wild cat. (**scared/daring**)

- The wind blew a ball of dust into my eye. (**ball/speck**)

4 Read each sentence and ask students to decide if it is true or false. If the sentence is false, instruct students to explain why.

- A speck can be hard to see. (**true**)

- To hush means to make a lot of noise. (**false; to hush means to get quiet**)

- A mountain climber is a daring person. (**true**)

- One way to find out about a place is to take a tour of it. (**true**)

Answers for page 67: 1. C, 2. G, 3. B, 4. J

Name _____

Review Words hush • daring • speck • tour

Fill in the bubble next to the correct answer.

1. When you *hush*, you ___.
- Ⓐ speak louder
- Ⓑ snoop around
- Ⓒ quiet down
- Ⓓ repeat words

2. Which sentence uses the word *daring* correctly?
- Ⓕ The daring children fell asleep right away.
- Ⓖ The daring girl learned how to walk a tightrope.
- Ⓗ Shelby is so daring that she always eats quickly.
- Ⓙ This daring picture shows a pretty waterfall.

3. Which is the size of a *speck*?
- Ⓐ a leaf
- Ⓑ a dot
- Ⓒ a balloon
- Ⓓ a rock

4. Which might you visit on a *tour*?
- Ⓕ a large closet
- Ⓖ the space under your bed
- Ⓗ the top of your kitchen table
- Ⓙ a store where they make candy

Writing

Write about someone who is daring. Use **daring** in your sentence.

_____

_____

fuss

noun

You make a **fuss** to show that you are upset about something.

Sam argued and made a **fuss** because he didn't want to wear gloves and a scarf to school.

Which sentences tell about someone who made a **fuss**?

- Roy threw the game pieces across the floor when he lost.
- The baby cried loudly when she was hungry.
- Chad shared his snack with Brian.
- Carmen complained when the puppy chewed on her new shoes.
- Hannah smiled after she read the book all by herself.

Think about times when you have made a **fuss**. What upset you? Are there times when it is not okay to make a **fuss**? When and why?

explore

verb

When you **explore**, you learn about something new.

David wants to **explore** the cave so he can see the strange animals that live inside it.

Which sentences tell about people who **explore**?

- John observes anthills to see how ants live.
- Stella dives deep into the ocean to learn how squids squirt ink.
- Dad drives the same way to work every day.
- Astronauts landed on the moon to learn how it is different from Earth.
- Carl watches the same movie over and over again.

What places in your neighorhood could you **explore**? What faraway places would you like to **explore**?

jolly

adjective

A **jolly** person is happy and full of fun.

My **jolly** Aunt Meg likes to laugh and have a good time.

Which are good reasons to feel **jolly**?

- It's your birthday and you're having a party.
- You are going to the dentist.
- You and your family are building a big sand castle at the beach.
- Your cat is very sick.
- Your uncle is telling you funny jokes.

Who is a **jolly** person you know?
How do you feel when you are with a **jolly** person?
What do you like about **jolly** people?

snicker

verb

When you laugh in a mean way, you **snicker**.

When her stepmom told Cinderella she could not go to the ball, Cinderella's stepsisters **snickered**.

Which words describe a person who **snickers**?

- kind
- friendly
- mean
- helps others
- makes fun of others

Why is it mean to **snicker**? How do you feel when someone **snickers**?

fuss • explore • jolly • snicker

Write on the board the four words studied this week. Read the words with the class and briefly review their meanings. Then conduct the oral activities below.

1 Tell students that you are going to give them a clue about one of the words for the week. They are to find the word that answers the clue.

- People do this when they laugh in a mean way. (**snicker**)

- If you were upset, you might make one. (**a fuss**)

- You could use this word to describe a very cheerful person. (**jolly**)

- Astronauts do this when they go to the moon. (**explore**)

2 Read each sentence and ask students to supply the correct word to complete the sentence.

- Mom makes a ____ when I throw my clothes on the closet floor. (**fuss**)

- It is mean to ____ when someone gives a wrong answer. (**snicker**)

- My ____ grandpa loves to tell jokes at the dinner table. (**jolly**)

- Divers wear special clothing that keeps them warm as they ____ the ocean. (**explore**)

3 Read each sentence and ask students to tell which word or words are wrong. Then have them provide the correct word from the week's list.

- The sad clown smiled and laughed as she skipped by in the parade. (**sad/jolly**)

- When someone accidentally falls down, it is not nice to offer help. (**offer help/snicker**)

- When we broke a window, Mom was so upset that she made a joke. (**joke/fuss**)

- Being in an exciting place makes me want to ignore it. (**ignore/explore**)

4 Read each sentence and ask students to decide if it is true or false. If the sentence is false, instruct students to explain why.

- A person who makes a fuss is calm and quiet. (**false; a person who makes a fuss is upset**)

- A jolly person is grumpy. (**false; a jolly person is happy**)

- Taking a tour is one way to explore a new city. (**true**)

- Snickering is happy laughter. (**false; snickering is mean laughter**)

Answers for page 71: 1. A, 2. J, 3. B, 4. H

Name _____

Review Words   fuss • explore • jolly • snicker

Fill in the bubble next to the correct answer.

1. What might you make a _fuss_ about?

Ⓐ Your baby sister tore up your homework.

Ⓑ Your mom cooked your favorite food for dinner.

Ⓒ Your teacher looked at your work and said "Good job!"

Ⓓ Your basketball team won the game.

2. When people _explore_, they look for ___.

Ⓕ things they've lost

Ⓖ new friends

Ⓗ something to do

Ⓙ new information

3. Who is _jolly_?

Ⓐ a person who is crying

Ⓑ a person who is laughing

Ⓒ a grouchy person

Ⓓ a person who is bored

4. What might someone say after _snickering_ at someone else?

Ⓕ "Are you okay?"

Ⓖ "Let me help you."

Ⓗ "What a dumb answer."

Ⓙ "Please tell me why you're sad."

Writing

Write about a place you would like to explore. Use **explore** in your sentence.

_____

_____

aim

noun

Your **aim** is a goal that you are willing to work for.

My **aim** for the weekend is to finish building my model boat.

Which are good **aims** for a six-year-old child?

- to learn how to drive a car
- to read 100 books in a month
- to learn how to count in Spanish
- to learn to play soccer
- to make new friends

What is your **aim** for the day? What is an **aim** that you are working on in first grade?

patient

adjective

A **patient** person does not get upset when things take a long time.

The **patient** teacher repeated the directions over and over until everyone knew what to do.

Which sentences tell about someone who is **patient**?

- Dad lets little Jessie tie her own shoes even though it takes her a while.
- Mary whines when she has to wait for her turn.
- Our coach keeps showing us how to hit a ball.
- Juan sits quietly until the doctor is ready to see him.
- Ben complains every time someone makes a mistake.

Who is a **patient** person you know? How can you tell that he or she is **patient**? How do you feel when you are with a **patient** person?

creep

verb

People who **creep** move carefully and quietly so that no one will see or hear them.

My brother likes to **creep** up behind me when I'm reading a book. Then he says "Boo!"

When might you **creep** along?

- when you want to surprise someone
- when there's a fire drill
- when you don't want to wake your dad
- when your mom is sick in bed
- when you're running a race

Show what people do when they **creep** along.
Tell about a time when you had to **creep** rather than walk normally.

drenched

adjective

Something is **drenched** when it is soaking wet.

My shoes were **drenched** from playing in rain puddles on my way home from school.

Which of the following would make you **drenched**?

- lying on a sunny beach
- jumping into a swimming pool
- taking a shower
- walking in a light snowfall
- walking in a rainstorm

Tell about a time when you were **drenched**. Do you like being **drenched**? Why or why not?

aim • patient • creep • drenched

Write on the board the four words studied this week. Read the words with the class and briefly review their meanings. Then conduct the oral activities below.

1 Tell students that you are going to give them a clue about one of the words for the week. They are to find the word that answers the clue.

- A superhero might do this to sneak up on a bad guy. (**creep**)

- This word describes someone who can wait calmly. (**patient**)

- This is a plan or goal. (**an aim**)

- This word describes a dog that has been playing in a rainstorm. (**drenched**)

2 Read each sentence and ask students to supply the correct word to complete the sentence.

- My ____ in first grade is to learn how to read. (**aim**)

- Danny likes to get ____ with a garden hose when it is hot outside. (**drenched**)

- I tried to ____ out the door without making a sound. (**creep**)

- Mom says we must be ____ with my baby brother while he is learning how to use a spoon. (**patient**)

3 Read each sentence and ask students to tell which word or words are wrong. Then have them provide the correct word from the week's list.

- The angry woman waited calmly for two hours to see her doctor. (**angry/patient**)

- My gloves were dry after I played for hours in the snow. (**dry/drenched**)

- Patrick began to stomp loudly out of the room so that no one would hear him. (**stomp loudly/creep**)

- My cousin hopes to become a firefighter someday—that is her job. (**job/aim**)

4 Read each sentence and ask students to decide if it is true or false. If the sentence is false, instruct students to explain why.

- People who snoop in other people's closets might creep around so they won't be caught. (**true**)

- Only grown-ups have aims. (**false; children have aims, too**)

- A patient person makes a fuss when he or she has to wait. (**false; a patient person waits calmly**)

- Water might drip from a drenched towel. (**true**)

Answers for page 75: 1. D, 2. G, 3. C, 4. F

Review Words   aim • patient • creep • drenched

Fill in the bubble next to the correct answer.

1. A *drenched* dog is very ___.
- Ⓐ playful
- Ⓑ small
- Ⓒ old
- Ⓓ wet

2. A *patient* person is someone who ___.
- Ⓕ hates to wait in long lines
- Ⓖ is willing to wait for things to happen
- Ⓗ is daring when it comes to trying scary new things
- Ⓙ gets upset about almost anything

3. What does it mean to *creep*?
- Ⓐ to move as fast as possible
- Ⓑ to watch something move
- Ⓒ to move slowly and quietly
- Ⓓ to jump as high as you can

4. Which sentence tells about an *aim*?
- Ⓕ I want to learn how to catch a fish.
- Ⓖ I can make a puppet out of a sock.
- Ⓗ I am very good at jumping rope.
- Ⓙ I can put this puzzle together.

Writing

Write about someone who got drenched. Use **drenched** in your sentence.

_____

_____

jumbo

adjective

Something that is **jumbo** is very big.

The **jumbo** burger at Fred's Burger House is big enough for three people.

Which of these could be described as **jumbo**?

- an elephant
- a toy airplane
- a ladybug
- a blue whale
- a jet plane

What are some other animals or things that could be described as **jumbo**?

Is it ever good to order the **jumbo** size of something?

dodge

verb

You **dodge** something by quickly getting out of its way.

I had to **dodge** a beach ball that was flying toward my head.

Which are ways to **dodge** a playground ball that is coming toward you?

- catch the ball
- move away from the ball
- duck so that the ball will go over your head
- jump out of the ball's way
- let the ball hit you

Show how to **dodge** something that is coming toward you. Have you ever had to **dodge** when you were playing dodgeball? Explain how you **dodged** the ball.

odd

adjective

Something is **odd** if it is strange or unusual.

A penguin is an **odd** bird because it does not fly.

Which of these would be **odd**?

- Your teacher comes to school in a bathing suit.
- There are no books in the library.
- A storybook has pictures in it.
- The cafeteria only serves ice cream and cookies for lunch.
- Your pencil needs to be sharpened.

What are some other things that would be **odd**?

deed

noun

When you do a good **deed**, you do something nice for someone.

My mom said I did a good **deed** when I let my little sister play with my friend and me.

Who is doing a good **deed**?

- Adam packs a lunch for his brother to take to school.
- Cathy leaves her toys all over the floor.
- Kristy quietly teases her brother so her dad doesn't hear.
- Jan helps her teacher erase the board.
- Darren helps a classmate find his lunch money in the grass.

What is a good **deed** that you have done? Why did you do that good **deed**? How did you feel after you did it?

jumbo • dodge • odd • deed

Write on the board the four words studied this week. Read the words with the class and briefly review their meanings. Then conduct the oral activities below.

❶ Tell students that you are going to give them a clue about one of the words for the week. They are to find the word that answers the clue.

- This word tells what you do to move quickly out of the way of something. **(dodge it)**

- This word means the same as *strange*. **(odd)**

- You might do this to help someone. **(a good deed)**

- This word describes the size of an elephant. **(jumbo)**

❷ Read each sentence and ask students to supply the correct word to complete the sentence.

- I try to do one good ____ a day. **(deed)**

- My mom surprised me with a ____ box of crayons that has 100 colors. **(jumbo)**

- An elephant has an ____ nose that reaches down to its toes! **(odd)**

- I had to ____ the ball so it wouldn't hit me. **(dodge)**

❸ Read each sentence and ask students to tell which word is wrong. Then have them provide the correct word from the week's list.

- The taxi driver tried to hit a squirrel that suddenly ran into the street. **(hit/dodge)**

- A small-sized bucket of chicken will feed ten people. **(small-/jumbo-)**

- It would be normal to have snow in August. **(normal/odd)**

❹ Read each sentence and ask students to decide if it is true or false. If the sentence is false, instruct students to explain why.

- Something that is jumbo is very small. **(false; things that are jumbo are very large)**

- It is odd to have a dog for a pet. **(false; it is common to have a dog for a pet)**

- Helping your mom fold the laundry is a good deed. **(true)**

- To dodge means to stand still. **(false; to dodge means to move quickly out of the way)**

Answers for page 79: 1. B, 2. F, 3. C, 4. J

Review Words	jumbo • dodge • odd • deed

Fill in the bubble next to the correct answer.

1. Which is *odd*?

Ⓐ a tree that loses its leaves

Ⓑ snow falling in the summer

Ⓒ a bird that lays eggs

Ⓓ a fish that swims

2. Which is a good *deed*?

Ⓕ feeding your pet so your dad doesn't have to

Ⓖ watching television for a few hours every day

Ⓗ writing with a pencil

Ⓙ buttoning your shirt

3. The word *jumbo* describes something that is ___.

Ⓐ very small in size

Ⓑ very hot to the touch

Ⓒ very large in size

Ⓓ very good to eat

4. To *dodge* means to ___.

Ⓕ stand as still as you can

Ⓖ laugh as loudly as you can

Ⓗ blow bubbles with bubble gum

Ⓙ move quickly out of the way

Writing ···

Write about something that is odd. Use **odd** in your sentence.

_____

_____

dangle

verb

Something **dangles** when it hangs down and swings loosely.

When I **dangle** a piece of yarn in front of my cat, she jumps up and grabs it.

Which of the following **dangle**?

- a birdhouse hanging from a tree branch
- your legs when you sit in a very tall chair
- keys on a key chain
- a dish on the table
- a worm on a fish hook

Take a piece of yarn or string and make it **dangle**. What do you see in the classroom that **dangles**?

equipment

noun

Equipment is a set of special things you need for a particular activity.

A tent and sleeping bags are some of the **equipment** we need to go camping.

What activity can you do with each set of **equipment**?

- paints, paintbrushes, easel, paper
- bats, balls, gloves
- face mask, flippers, swimsuit
- kneepads, elbow pads, skateboard
- hammer, nails, wood, saw

What **equipment** does your school have that helps you learn? What **equipment** does your school have for playing during recess?

peppy

adjective

A **peppy** person or animal is full of energy.

My **peppy** baby sister jumped up and down in her crib.

Who was feeling **peppy**?

- Talia whistled while she planted flowers.
- Jeremy spent the afternoon jumping on a trampoline.
- Uncle Ron sat and worked on a crossword puzzle.
- Amanda did not want to get out of bed.
- Bosco the dog played fetch-the-bone for an hour.

When do you feel **peppy**? What do you like to do when you feel **peppy**?

stroll

verb

When you **stroll**, you take a slow, relaxed walk.

Gina likes to take her time and **stroll** past the animals when she goes to the zoo.

When are good times to **stroll**?

- when you need to catch the school bus
- when you have a lot of free time
- when you are running a race
- when you are playing tag
- when you are pushing a baby in a stroller

Tell about a time when you **strolled** around somewhere. Where is a good place to **stroll**?
Show your classmates how to **stroll** across the room.

dangle • equipment • peppy • stroll

Write on the board the four words studied this week. Read the words with the class and briefly review their meanings. Then conduct the oral activities below.

1 Tell students that you are going to give them a clue about one of the words for the week. They are to find the word that answers the clue.

- You can use this word to describe a playful kitten. **(peppy)**

- This word tells what your feet do when you swing on a swing. **(dangle)**

- You might do this if you wanted to walk slowly. **(stroll)**

- This is a word for all of the things you need to play a sport. **(equipment)**

2 Read each sentence and ask students to supply the correct word to complete the sentence.

- Josh likes to climb onto a tree branch and ____ his legs. **(dangle)**

- Firefighters use a lot of ____ to fight fires. **(equipment)**

- The ____ fans jumped up and cheered loudly when their team won. **(peppy)**

- Simon likes to take his time and ____ along the beach. **(stroll)**

3 Read each sentence and ask students to tell which word or words are wrong. Then have them provide the correct word from the week's list.

- Let's race through the dinosaur museum to make sure we don't miss a thing. **(race/stroll)**

- The tired puppy jumped and ran and chased her tail. **(tired/peppy)**

- Hoses, ladders, and axes are some of the toys that firefighters use. **(toys/equipment)**

- You sit on your legs when you swing on a swing. **(sit on/dangle)**

4 Read each sentence and ask students to decide if it is true or false. If the sentence is false, instruct students to explain why.

- The word *peppy* means about the same as *poky*. **(false; someone who is peppy is full of energy; someone who is poky moves slowly)**

- Strolling helps runners to win races. **(false; a runner cannot win a race by walking slowly)**

- Your legs dangle when you ride a Ferris wheel. **(true)**

- Golf balls, basketballs, and soccer balls are sports equipment. **(true)**

Answers for page 83: 1. B, 2. H, 3. D, 4. F

Name _____

Fill in the bubble next to the correct answer.

1. Which word means about the same as *peppy*?

Ⓐ sleepy

Ⓑ frisky

Ⓒ gloomy

Ⓓ scared

2. Which one *dangles*?

Ⓕ a car in a parking lot

Ⓖ a bowl of soup

Ⓗ a long earring

Ⓙ a glass of milk

3. Football *equipment* includes ____.

Ⓐ lots of energy

Ⓑ cheering fans

Ⓒ lots of practice

Ⓓ helmets and shoulder pads

4. When you *stroll,* you ____.

Ⓕ walk slowly

Ⓖ skip and hop

Ⓗ are in a hurry

Ⓙ march in place

Writing

Write about a peppy person. Use **peppy** in your sentence.

_____

_____

panic

verb

When you **panic**, you become very afraid and don't know what to do.

The people inside the elevator began to **panic** when the door would not open.

In which situation might you **panic**?

- The fire alarm goes off while you are sleeping.
- You see a large snake on the path in front of you.
- You are eating pizza with a friend.
- You get lost at the zoo.
- You are cheering for your favorite team.

Did you ever **panic**? What caused you to **panic**?

interest

noun

You have an **interest** in something if you want to know more about it.

When he was my age, my dad showed an **interest** in playing the guitar.

How does someone show **interest** in a subject?

- by looking bored
- by asking questions about it
- by reading books about it
- by talking about it
- by acting sleepy when someone else talks about it

What do you have an **interest** in? How can you find out more about it? Does anyone in your family share this **interest** with you?

final

adjective

Something that is **final** comes at the end.

We will go home early on the **final** day of school.

Which of the following are **final**?

- the last page in a book
- the beginning of a story
- the last word in a dictionary
- the last car on a train
- the first scene in a movie

Tell about the **final** page in a book you like or the **final** scene in a movie you like.

direct

verb

When you **direct** someone, you tell that person how to get somewhere.

Can you please **direct** me to the principal's office?

Which words mean about the same as **direct**?

- give directions
- show the way
- ask for directions
- lead the way
- turn around

Show how you would **direct** someone from your classroom to the kindergarten room. Show how you would **direct** someone from your classroom to the playground.

panic • interest • final • direct

Write on the board the four words studied this week. Read the words with the class and briefly review their meanings. Then conduct the oral activities below.

1 Tell students that you are going to give them a clue about one of the words for the week. They are to find the word that answers the clue.

- You might need to do this for someone who is lost. (**direct that person**)

- You might do this if you were in a small boat on the ocean when a big storm began. (**panic**)

- This word means *last*. (**final**)

- This word names something you would like to know more about. (**an interest**)

2 Read each sentence and ask students to supply the correct word to complete the sentence.

- Katie began to _____ when she got lost in the forest. (**panic**)

- My team plays one _____ baseball game and then the season is over. (**final**)

- I need someone to _____ me to the airport so I can catch a plane. (**direct**)

- Heather has an _____ in rocks of all different colors, shapes, and sizes. (**interest**)

3 Read each sentence and ask students to tell which word or words are wrong. Then have them provide the correct word from the week's list.

- "I'm looking for a motel," said the tourist. "Can you confuse me?" (**confuse/direct**)

- Tori began to calm down when she saw the tornado moving toward her house. (**calm down/panic**)

- The first leaf has fallen off the tree and now the tree is bare. (**first/final**)

- "I love flowers! They are one of my main dislikes." (**dislikes/interests**)

4 Read each sentence and ask students to decide if it is true or false. If the sentence is false, instruct students to explain why.

- To direct someone is to tell that person how to get somewhere. (**true**)

- Some writers write "The End" on the final page of their stories. (**true**)

- It is fun to learn about things that you have an interest in. (**true**)

- When you panic, you calmly decide what to do. (**false; you are so scared that you don't know what to do**)

Answers for page 87: 1. B, 2. J, 3. D, 4. H

Review Words   panic • interest • final • direct

Fill in the bubble next to the correct answer.

1. How might someone show an *interest* in cooking?
- Ⓐ by eating three meals a day
- Ⓑ by reading lots of cookbooks
- Ⓒ by setting the table every night
- Ⓓ by thanking Grandma for a good meal

2. Why might Mandy *panic*?
- Ⓕ She did all of her homework.
- Ⓖ She made a special gift for her mom.
- Ⓗ She patted her cat's soft, fluffy fur.
- Ⓙ She left her purse at the mall.

3. Which is the *final* month of the year?
- Ⓐ January
- Ⓑ June
- Ⓒ May
- Ⓓ December

4. To *direct* someone means that you ____.
- Ⓕ turn the person around a few times
- Ⓖ tell the person all about your pet
- Ⓗ tell the person the way to go
- Ⓙ sing a song with the person

Writing

Write about an interest you have. Use **interest** in your sentence.

_____

_____

sniff

verb

When you **sniff**, you take short breaths through your nose.

Sniff this shampoo and tell me if you like the way it smells.

Which can you figure out by **sniffing**?

- how yummy popcorn smells
- how bumpy a toad's skin is
- how many colors there are in a rainbow
- whether something is burning in the oven
- when it's time to take out the garbage

What things do you like to **sniff**? What things would you rather not **sniff**? Show your classmates how to **sniff**.

collection

noun

A **collection** is a group of things that are alike.

Emily has large and small seashells in her shell **collection**.

Which of the following children have **collections**?

- Matt has a toy fox.
- Jeremy has a lot of small toy cars.
- Maria has a doll, a schoolbook, and a ball.
- Stan has coins from around the world.
- Stacy owns ten dolls.

Do you have a **collection**? Tell about your **collection**. How do you collect things for your **collection**?

wander

verb

You **wander** when you walk around without a purpose or a plan.

Jake decided to **wander** around the mall until it was time for the movie to start.

Who might **wander**?

- a student walking home from school
- a runner nearing the finish line
- someone who is visiting a beach for the first time
- someone who likes to stroll around
- a sick person who needs to get to the hospital

Do you and your family ever **wander** around together? Where is a good place to **wander**? When is a good time to **wander**?

flabbergasted

adjective

A **flabbergasted** person is surprised and amazed.

April was **flabbergasted** when she opened the door and heard everyone yell "Surprise!"

Would you be **flabbergasted** if you saw someone:

- dance with a tiger?
- eat a sandwich?
- ride an elephant to school?
- climb a mountain of ice?
- walk a dog on a leash?

Tell about a time when you were **flabbergasted**.

sniff • collection • wander • flabbergasted

Write on the board the four words studied this week. Read the words with the class and briefly review their meanings. Then conduct the oral activities below.

1 Tell students that you are going to give them a clue about one of the words for the week. They are to find the word that answers the clue.

- Some people do this in shopping malls when they aren't in a hurry. **(wander)**

- This word describes someone who is very surprised. **(flabbergasted)**

- You use your nose to do this. **(sniff)**

- This is a group of things that you collect, or save. **(a collection)**

2 Read each sentence and ask students to supply the correct word to complete the sentence.

- People often ____ when they have colds. **(sniff)**

- Jamie was ____ to hear that she had won a brand-new bike! **(flabbergasted)**

- Our classroom library has a large ____ of books. **(collection)**

- Jimmy likes to ____ through the rooms of his grandmother's large house. **(wander)**

3 Read each sentence and ask students to tell which word is wrong. Then have them provide the correct word from the week's list.

- The museum has many huge dinosaur bones in its kitchen. **(kitchen/collection)**

- My dog Ariel likes to taste her food before she takes a bite. **(taste/sniff)**

- We have plenty of time, so let's rush through the aquarium and see all the fish. **(rush/wander)**

- Mia was bored when she saw a gray whale leap out of the ocean. **(bored/flabbergasted)**

4 Read each sentence and ask students to decide if it is true or false. If the sentence is false, instruct students to explain why.

- One book can be a collection. **(false; a collection is a group of things)**

- You wander when you walk directly from one place to another place. **(false; you wander when you walk around without a plan)**

- You use your ears to sniff a flower. **(false; you use your nose to sniff)**

- *Flabbergasted* and *amazed* have about the same meaning. **(true)**

Answers for page 91: 1. A, 2. H, 3. B, 4. G

Review Words	sniff • collection • wander • flabbergasted

Fill in the bubble next to the correct answer.

1. Which means about the same as *sniff*?

Ⓐ smell

Ⓑ touch

Ⓒ hear

Ⓓ see

2. Which is a *collection*?

Ⓕ everything in your kitchen

Ⓖ your family's television set

Ⓗ ten stuffed animals on your sister's bed

Ⓙ your favorite stuffed animal, a horse named Star

3. When you *wander,* you ___.

Ⓐ run as fast as you can

Ⓑ walk without a plan

Ⓒ walk to school

Ⓓ stay in one place

4. Which might make you feel *flabbergasted*?

Ⓕ washing your face in the morning

Ⓖ watching a butterfly come out of a cocoon

Ⓗ watching your mom cook dinner for the family

Ⓙ watching the same movie over and over

Writing

Write about a time when you felt flabbergasted. Use **flabbergasted** in your sentence.

_____

_____

hobby

noun

A **hobby** is something that you like to do for fun.

On Saturdays, Mark enjoys his **hobby** of building wooden birdhouses.

Which of the following might be a **hobby**?

- making things out of clay
- building model cars or planes
- doing the laundry
- creating stuffed teddy bears
- putting toys away in your closet

Tell about one of your **hobbies**. Tell about a **hobby** you would like to have.

rustle

verb

Things **rustle** when they rub together and make a soft crackling sound.

When a breeze blows through a tree, its leaves **rustle**.

Which would **rustle**?

- a cat moving inside a paper grocery bag
- water dripping from a faucet
- a doorbell ringing
- a small dog running across fallen leaves
- a car horn beeping

Rustle some papers together to make a rustling sound. What other things in the classroom **rustle** when you rub them together?

appreciate

verb

When you **appreciate** something, you are thankful for it.

I **appreciate** the movies you gave me to watch while I was sick.

Which are ways to say that you **appreciate** a gift?

- "Thank you!"
- "I don't want this."
- "It was nice of you to give me a gift."
- "I'm sorry."
- "What a wonderful gift this is!"

What are some things people do for you that you **appreciate**? What are some things you do for others that they **appreciate**?

nutritious

adjective

Nutritious food has vitamins and other things that you need to stay healthy.

Fresh fruits and vegetables are **nutritious** foods that people should eat every day.

Which of the foods in each pair is **nutritious**?

- cotton candy or carrots?
- bananas or bubble gum?
- soda or milk?
- peas or potato chips?
- corn or a candy bar?

Name some of your favorite **nutritious** foods and drinks.

hobby • rustle • appreciate • nutritious

Write on the board the four words studied this week. Read the words with the class and briefly review their meanings. Then conduct the oral activities below.

1 Tell students that you are going to give them a clue about one of the words for the week. They are to find the word that answers the clue.

- This word can be used to describe green beans, broccoli, and oranges. **(nutritious)**

- Paper grocery bags do this when you fold or unfold them. **(rustle)**

- You might use this word when you thank someone. **(appreciate)**

- This is an activity that you do for fun. **(a hobby)**

2 Read each sentence and ask students to supply the correct word to complete the sentence.

- My mom's ___ is sewing pretty quilts. **(hobby)**

- I ___ it when students help me pass out supplies. **(appreciate)**

- I could hear the wrapping paper ___ as Julia wrapped a present. **(rustle)**

- Children need ___ food because their bones and bodies are growing. **(nutritious)**

3 Read each sentence and ask students to tell which word or words are wrong. Then have them provide the correct word from the week's list.

- Tommy's job is collecting baseball cards to trade with his friends. **(job/hobby)**

- When you pick up a potato chip bag, the chips bang against one another. **(bang/rustle)**

- Raisins, cheese, and apples are unhealthy snacks. **(unhealthy/nutritious)**

- I don't care about your hard work on the class project. **(don't care about/appreciate)**

4 Read each sentence and ask students to decide if it is true or false. If the sentence is false, instruct students to explain why.

- A hobby is something you enjoy and show interest in. **(true)**

- Your hands rustle when you clap them together. **(false; when things rustle, they make a soft sound)**

- *Nutritious* means *healthy*. **(true)**

- If someone did a good deed for you, you'd probably appreciate it. **(true)**

Answers for page 95: 1. C, 2. H, 3. D, 4. F

A Word a Day • EMC 2791 • © Evan-Moor Corp.

Review Words	hobby • rustle • appreciate • nutritious

Fill in the bubble next to the correct answer.

1. Which are *nutritious*?
Ⓐ good books
Ⓑ your favorite toys
Ⓒ healthy foods
Ⓓ colorful shirts

2. When leaves *rustle* in the wind, they ___.
Ⓕ make a loud, scary noise
Ⓖ change color
Ⓗ make a soft sound
Ⓙ grow bigger

3. A *hobby* is ___.
Ⓐ a project you do in school
Ⓑ a chore you do at home
Ⓒ a good deed you do for someone
Ⓓ something that you love to do

4. When you *appreciate* something, you feel ___.
Ⓕ thankful
Ⓖ sleepy
Ⓗ mad
Ⓙ sorry

Writing

Write about someone you appreciate. Use **appreciate** in your sentence.

_____

_____

sample

noun

A **sample** is a small amount of something that shows what the rest is like.

Michael asked for a **sample** of rocky-road ice cream so he could find out if he liked the flavor.

Why might a store give free **samples**?

- so shoppers will try products
- so shoppers will buy larger amounts next time
- to do a good deed
- to make money

Have you ever been in a supermarket when someone was giving out free **samples** of food to shoppers? What foods were they letting people taste?

Tell about other **samples** that you have seen at home or in stores.

dazzle

verb

You **dazzle** people when you amaze and impress them.

The ice skater **dazzled** the audience when she jumped into the air and twirled around.

What might you say to someone who **dazzled** you?

- "Wow! You're amazing!"
- "That's the most incredible performance I've ever seen!"
- "That's easy—anyone can do that!"
- "How in the world did you do that?"
- "That's boring!"

Tell about someone you saw who **dazzled** you.
Think of something you could do that might **dazzle** people.

flutter

verb

Something **flutters** when it quickly flaps up and down or from side to side.

A butterfly **flutters** its wings when it flies.

Which might **flutter**?

- a bird's wings
- a flag flapping in the breeze
- a turtle crawling across the sand
- a kite's tail
- a cat jumping onto a table

Open one of your books and make the pages **flutter**. Use your hand to show what fluttering looks like.

sensible

adjective

Sensible people think carefully and make wise choices.

Austin decided that it wouldn't be **sensible** to walk across the frozen pond.

Which are **sensible** actions?

- Wearing gloves and a scarf when it's snowing
- Doing your homework at bedtime
- Staying away from dogs you don't know
- Not carrying a chocolate bar in your pocket on a hot day
- Never going to bed before ten o'clock at night

Tell about a **sensible** decision you made. Why did you make that **sensible** decision?

sample • dazzle • flutter • sensible

Write on the board the four words studied this week. Read the words with the class and briefly review their meanings. Then conduct the oral activities below.

1 Tell students that you are going to give them a clue about one of the words for the week. They are to find the word that answers the clue.

- This is another word for *amaze*. **(dazzle)**

- A bug's wings do this. **(flutter)**

- This is a small taste of food. **(a sample)**

- This word describes a person who makes wise choices. **(sensible)**

2 Read each sentence and ask students to supply the correct word to complete the sentence.

- It is ____ to stay home in bed and rest when you are sick. **(sensible)**

- Maddy blinked quickly, making her eyelashes ____. **(flutter)**

- The magician promised to ____ the audience by making an elephant disappear. **(dazzle)**

- The doctor will take a ____ of my blood to make sure that I'm healthy. **(sample)**

3 Read each sentence and ask students to tell which word is wrong. Then have them provide the correct word from the week's list.

- Calling your mom to say that you will be late is a silly thing to do. **(silly/sensible)**

- A hummingbird flattens its wings as it searches for food. **(flattens/flutters)**

- The juggler says he will bore us by juggling ten different vegetables at once. **(bore/dazzle)**

4 Read each sentence and ask students to decide if it is true or false. If the sentence is false, instruct students to explain why.

- A sample is a small piece or amount. **(true)**

- Skateboarders might dazzle you with the tricks they do. **(true)**

- On a snowy day, it would be sensible to wear a bathing suit outdoors. **(false; it is not wise to wear a bathing suit outdoors in the snow)**

- You can flutter your arms the way a bird flutters its wings. **(true)**

Answers for page 99: 1. D, 2. H, 3. A, 4. G

Name _____

Fill in the bubble next to the correct answer.

1. Which body part does a bird *flutter*?

- Ⓐ its claws
- Ⓑ its feet
- Ⓒ its ears
- Ⓓ its wings

2. What might *dazzle* a crowd at the beach?

- Ⓕ a sea gull flying by
- Ⓖ the warm sand
- Ⓗ a dolphin jumping out of the water
- Ⓙ the sound of the waves

3. Which sentence uses the word *sample* correctly?

- Ⓐ The sample of cherry juice came in a small paper cup.
- Ⓑ The boxes will sample if you stack them too high.
- Ⓒ You can sample the papers together with a paper clip.
- Ⓓ A large sample of people is waiting to see the movie.

4. Which animal in *The Three Little Pigs* is most *sensible*?

- Ⓕ the pig who makes a house out of straw
- Ⓖ the pig who builds a strong brick house
- Ⓗ the pig who makes a house out of sticks
- Ⓙ the wolf who tries to catch the pigs

Writing

Tell about a way you could dazzle your friends. Use **dazzle** in your sentence.

_____

_____

skill

noun

A **skill** is the ability to do something well.

Playing the piano is a **skill** that takes a lot of practice.

Which activities require having a **skill**?

- taking a nap
- reading a story to a friend
- jumping with a jump-rope
- skiing down a hill
- eating a sandwich

Tell about one of your **skills**. Tell about a **skill** that you would like to have. How can you learn that new **skill**?

nimble

adjective

A **nimble** person or animal moves quickly and easily.

The **nimble** goat jumped from rock to rock without slipping.

Which of the following are examples of being **nimble**?

- My cat dashes through the grass without making a sound.
- The ballet dancer gracefully leaps and twirls.
- The alligator crawls slowly into the swamp.
- My brother slipped when he reached first base.
- Missy falls a lot when she goes roller-skating.

What sports need **nimble** players?
For what activities do people need **nimble** hands and fingers?

zip

verb

When something **zips**, it moves fast.

The antelope **zipped** across the plain to escape the hungry lion.

Which words mean about the same as **zip**?

- dash
- rush
- stroll
- zoom
- creep

Do you like to **zip** along? When is a good time to **zip** down the sidewalk?

Show your classmates how to **zip** across the room.

mighty

adjective

A **mighty** person or thing is strong and powerful.

The lion gave a **mighty** roar that shook the leaves on the trees.

Which do you think are **mighty** animals?

- a kitten
- a Tyrannosaurus Rex
- a grizzly bear
- a tiger
- a goat

Have you ever seen someone who is **mighty**? What could that **mighty** person do? Who are some **mighty** cartoon characters?

skill • nimble • zip • mighty

Write on the board the four words studied this week. Read the words with the class and briefly review their meanings. Then conduct the oral activities below.

1 Tell students that you are going to give them a clue about one of the words for the week. They are to find the word that answers the clue.

- Runners do this when they are trying to win a race. (**zip**)

- Drawing is one. Dancing is another. (**a skill**)

- This word describes someone who is strong enough to lift a car. (**mighty**)

- A rabbit needs to be this way to run away quickly from dogs and foxes. (**nimble**)

2 Read each sentence and ask students to supply the correct word to complete the sentence.

- The ____ wind knocked down fences, trees, and power lines. (**mighty**)

- Maddy has learned the ____ of riding a two-wheeled bike. (**skill**)

- Noah's ____ fingers moved quickly over the piano keys as he played a song. (**nimble**)

- Roller coasters ____ up, down, and around their tracks at fast speeds. (**zip**)

3 Read each sentence and ask students to tell which word is wrong. Then have them provide the correct word from the week's list.

- The clumsy boy walked across the log without falling into the river. (**clumsy/nimble**)

- The weak wrestler lifted the big object up over his head. (**weak/mighty**)

- Firefighters creep to burning buildings so they can quickly put out the flames. (**creep/zip**)

- Typing is an important hobby for people who work with computers. (**hobby/skill**)

4 Read each sentence and ask students to decide if it is true or false. If the sentence is false, instruct students to explain why.

- A snail zips along the ground. (**false; a snail does not move quickly**)

- Reading is a skill that takes practice. (**true**)

- A grown-up gorilla is a mighty ape. (**true**)

- A nimble person often bumps into things. (**false; a nimble person moves easily**)

Answers for page 103: 1. C, 2. G, 3. A, 4. J

Review Words   skill • nimble • zip • mighty

Fill in the bubble next to the correct answer.

1. When is a good time to _zip_ around?
- Ⓐ while you are sleeping
- Ⓑ when you meet someone new
- Ⓒ when you are playing tag
- Ⓓ while you are eating

2. Which is _mighty_?
- Ⓕ a baby
- Ⓖ a giant
- Ⓗ a light breeze
- Ⓙ a soap bubble

3. Which is a _skill_?
- Ⓐ following directions
- Ⓑ breathing
- Ⓒ growing
- Ⓓ losing your baby teeth

4. Which sentence uses the word _nimble_ correctly?
- Ⓕ The nimble cook keeps dropping dishes on the floor.
- Ⓖ Max can nimble faster than his brother.
- Ⓗ Please hand me a nimble from that shelf.
- Ⓙ No one could catch the nimble soccer player.

Writing

Write about a time when you need to zip around. Use **zip** in your sentence.

_____

_____

vehicle

noun

People ride in **vehicles** and use them for moving things.

Cars, buses, bicycles, and trains are kinds of **vehicles** that go on land.

What **vehicles** might you see:

- high up in space?
- on a sidewalk?
- in a garage?
- on an ocean?
- on a highway?

What kind of **vehicle** would you like to invent? What would that **vehicle** do? What would that **vehicle** look like?

horrible

adjective

Something that is **horrible** is very bad.

I had a **horrible** cold that made my head ache, my nose run, and my throat sore.

Which words mean about the same as **horrible**?

- wonderful
- awful
- great
- terrible
- marvelous

What kinds of things might happen to make a day **horrible**?

peer

verb

You **peer** when you look very hard at something to see it better.

Sean **peered** into the aquarium full of fish and tried to find the tiny snail.

Which might you **peer** through in order to see something better?

- a magnifying glass
- a pair of binoculars
- a curtain
- a telescope
- a mask

Peer at a map or globe, or out the classroom window.
Name one thing that you see.
Show your classmates how to **peer** at something.

wealthy

adjective

A **wealthy** person has a lot of money.

Our **wealthy** neighbors own three cars, two boats, and a house on an island.

Which of these are probably **wealthy**?

- a family that owns an airplane
- someone who has only one pair of shoes
- a person who lives in a huge, fancy house
- people who buy all their clothes at thrift shops
- a family that has a swimming pool in the backyard

What would you do to help others if you were **wealthy**?

vehicle • horrible • peer • wealthy

Write on the board the four words studied this week. Read the words with the class and briefly review their meanings. Then conduct the oral activities below.

1 Tell students that you are going to give them a clue about one of the four words for the week. They are to find the word that answers the clue.

- A spaceship is one of these. (**a vehicle**)

- This word means the opposite of *very poor*. (**wealthy**)

- You might do this if you were trying to read tiny handwriting. (**peer at it**)

- You could use this word to describe a very bad odor. (**horrible**)

2 Read each sentence and ask students to supply the correct word to complete the sentence.

- Some ____ people gave money to build a computer lab for our school. (**wealthy**)

- Jenny woke up crying because she had a ____ nightmare about sharks with feet. (**horrible**)

- Gramps uses a magnifying glass to ____ at the map. (**peer**)

- That large ____ carries trash to the recycling center. (**vehicle**)

3 Read each sentence and ask students to tell which word or words are wrong. Then have them provide the correct word from the week's list.

- I had such a wonderful toothache that I had to see my dentist right away. (**wonderful/horrible**)

- We yelled into the thick fog, trying to see the road ahead. (**yelled/peered**)

- The Smiths are poor enough to give thousands of dollars to homeless people. (**poor/wealthy**)

- A sled is a warm coat for traveling across the snow. (**warm coat/vehicle**)

4 Read each sentence and ask students to decide if it is true or false. If the sentence is false, instruct students to explain why.

- Horrible news makes you smile. (**false; very bad news would not make you smile**)

- Some vehicles travel on land, and some vehicles fly through the air. (**true**)

- Most people peer at large signs that are easy to read. (**false; people peer at things that are hard to see**)

- The word *wealthy* means *very rich*. (**true**)

Answers for page 107: 1. B, 2. H, 3. D, 4. G

Review Words	vehicle • horrible • peer • wealthy

Fill in the bubble next to the correct answer.

1. Which word means the opposite of *wealthy*?

Ⓐ happy

Ⓑ poor

Ⓒ healthy

Ⓓ sad

2. What do most people use *vehicles* for?

Ⓕ sleeping

Ⓖ housecleaning

Ⓗ traveling

Ⓙ cooking

3. When might you need to *peer* around a room?

Ⓐ when it's morning

Ⓑ when the light is on

Ⓒ when it's noontime

Ⓓ when it's dark

4. Which means the opposite of *horrible*?

Ⓕ awful

Ⓖ wonderful

Ⓗ really terrible

Ⓙ okay, but not great

Writing

Write about a vehicle you would like to own. Use **vehicle** in your sentence.

_____

_____

yelp

verb

You **yelp** when you cry out quickly and sharply in pain.

The puppy **yelped** when Chris accidentally stepped on its paw.

When might you **yelp**?

- when you are stung by a bee
- when you eat a hamburger
- when you step barefoot on a tack
- when you feel like you're going to fall
- when you draw a picture

Tell about a time when you **yelped** or you heard a **yelp**. **Yelp** for your classmates.

swift

adjective

Something that is **swift** moves very quickly.

A **swift** wind quickly blew the sailboats out to sea.

Which words mean about the same as **swift**?

- poky
- quick
- speedy
- slow
- fast

What is something **swift** that flies through the air? Tell about some **swift** animals.

cluster

noun

A **cluster** is a number of things of the same kind that grow or are grouped close together.

Mom tucked a small **cluster** of green grapes into my lunchbox.

Which of the following can grow in **clusters**?

- pencils
- flowers
- stars
- grass
- bananas

Do you ever form a **cluster** with your teammates before you play a game? What do you do and say after forming a **cluster** with them? Form a **cluster** with some of your classmates.

gnaw

verb

You **gnaw** on something when you chew on it again and again.

My dog loves to **gnaw** on toy bones I buy at the pet store.

Which foods can you **gnaw**?

- a scoop of ice cream
- a cup of yogurt
- barbecued ribs
- a piece of hard cheese
- a carrot

Pretend that you are a dog **gnawing** on a bone. Which of your teeth do you use for **gnawing**?

yelp • swift • cluster • gnaw

Write on the board the four words studied this week. Read the words with the class and briefly review their meanings. Then conduct the oral activities below.

1 Tell students that you are going to give them a clue about one of the four words for the week. They are to find the word that answers the clue.

- This word describes a fast-moving jet plane. (**swift**)

- This is another word for *bunch* or *group*. (**cluster**)

- Dogs do this to bones. (**gnaw on them**)

- You might do this if someone pinched you. (**yelp**)

2 Read each sentence and ask students to supply the correct word to complete the sentence.

- The bride carried a ____ of purple and white flowers. (**cluster**)

- Marty heard his dog ____ when it was stung by a bee. (**yelp**)

- The mouse did not see the ____ owl as it swooped down from the sky. (**swift**)

- It's bad for your teeth to ____ on a pencil. (**gnaw**)

3 Read each sentence and ask students to tell which word or words are wrong. Then have them provide the correct word from the week's list.

- The slow rabbit escaped from a fox. (**slow/swift**)

- I could hear Jessie laugh when she stubbed her toe on a rock. (**laugh/yelp**)

- A rat can use its sharp teeth to lick a rope in half. (**lick/gnaw**)

- Penguins form a single line to keep warm. (**single line/cluster**)

4 Read each sentence and ask students to decide if it is true or false. If the sentence is false, instruct students to explain why.

- You make a sharp, crying sound when you yelp. (**true**)

- A hamster might gnaw on a carrot. (**true**)

- One grape is the same as a cluster. (**false; a cluster is a group of things**)

- Snails and turtles are swift animals. (**false; they aren't fast-moving animals**)

Answers for page 111: 1. B, 2. F, 3. C, 4. H

Review Words	yelp • swift • cluster • gnaw

Fill in the bubble next to the correct answer.

1. Which sentence tells about a *swift* person?
- (A) Ben moves slowly because he walks with crutches.
- (B) Briana is the fastest runner in our whole school.
- (C) Hannah takes her time when she eats her lunch.
- (D) Alexander can stand on one leg for one minute.

2. To *gnaw* means ____.
- (F) to chew again and again
- (G) to swallow slowly
- (H) to sip quickly
- (J) to take one bite

3. When you *yelp,* you ____.
- (A) giggle loudly
- (B) sing a song
- (C) cry out in pain
- (D) do not say a word

4. Which of the following makes up a *cluster*?
- (F) a bumblebee flying from flower to flower
- (G) pebbles scattered all over the road
- (H) children sitting in a group on the floor
- (J) library books lined up on a shelf

Writing

Write about a swift vehicle, person, or animal. Use **swift** in your sentence.

_____

_____

garment

noun

A **garment** is a piece of clothing.

Kelly likes to play dress-up and wear a **garment** that is too big for her.

Which of the following are **garments**?

- jeans
- shoes
- cellphones
- T-shirts
- wristwatches

Tell about your favorite **garment** and describe its texture. When do you like to wear your favorite **garment**?

scowl

verb

When you **scowl**, you make an angry frown.

My mom and dad **scowl** whenever I tease my little brother.

When might you **scowl**?

- when your friends clap for you
- when someone takes your toys without asking
- when you win a game
- when your pencil breaks while you are taking a test
- when you open your lunchbox and see your favorite foods inside

What makes you **scowl**? What makes grown-ups **scowl**?

Scowl for your classmates.

prance

verb

When you **prance**, you move around happily and proudly.

Andy began to **prance** around the field after he scored the winning goal for his soccer team.

When might you **prance**?

- when you fall and hurt your knee
- when you hit a home run
- when you are sick in bed with the flu
- when you win a spelling contest
- when you are lost in a big store

Have you ever seen a dog or horse **prance**? How did they look while they were **prancing**? Show your classmates how to **prance**.

thoughtful

adjective

A **thoughtful** person thinks about other people's feelings and needs.

It was so **thoughtful** of you to make me a get-well card when I was sick.

Which words mean about the same as **thoughtful**?

- selfish
- kind
- caring
- mean
- helpful

Tell about a **thoughtful** thing someone did for you. What is something **thoughtful** that you can do for someone today?

garment • scowl • prance • thoughtful

Write on the board the four words studied this week. Read the words with the class and briefly review their meanings. Then conduct the oral activities below.

1 Tell students that you are going to give them a clue about one of the four words for the week. They are to find the word that answers the clue.

- You might move this way if you were very proud of yourself. **(prance)**

- A shirt is one. **(a garment)**

- Your eyebrows wrinkle up when you do this. **(scowl)**

- This word describes a person who is kind to others. **(thoughtful)**

2 Read each sentence and ask students to supply the correct word to complete the sentence.

- Will saw his teacher ____ when the girls did not line up quietly. **(scowl)**

- My dog Biscuit will ____ around the yard when she's feeling happy. **(prance)**

- It was ____ of Jon to give me his sweater to wear when I was cold. **(thoughtful)**

- Mrs. Wolski held up a sweatshirt and asked, "Whose ____ is this?" **(garment)**

3 Read each sentence and ask students to tell which word is wrong. Then have them provide the correct word from the week's list.

- Shelly often wears a cape, which is a sheet without sleeves that hangs over her shoulders. **(sheet/garment)**

- It was so mean of Manuel to help me carry the groceries into the house. **(mean/thoughtful)**

- Jill was so pleased with her new outfit that she began to creep around the room. **(creep/prance)**

- I smile when I'm in a bad mood. **(smile/scowl)**

4 Read each sentence and ask students to decide if it is true or false. If the sentence is false, instruct students to explain why.

- People scowl to show how happy they are. **(false; people scowl when they are angry)**

- After the ballgame, the losers usually prance around the field. **(false; people prance around when they are proud and happy)**

- A thoughtful person makes a good friend. **(true)**

- Most garments are made of cloth. **(true)**

Answers for page 115: 1. C, 2. G, 3. A, 4. F

Name _____

Fill in the bubble next to the correct answer.

1. Which is a good *garment* to wear on a snowy day?

Ⓐ a sled

Ⓑ a snowman

Ⓒ a warm jacket

Ⓓ a cup of hot chocolate

2. Which sentence uses the word *thoughtful* correctly?

Ⓕ Brady's head was full of thoughtful.

Ⓖ The thoughtful child shared her snack with the new student.

Ⓗ My thoughtful is that we should go to see a movie.

Ⓙ The thoughtful dog gnawed on his juicy bone.

3. When you *prance*, you ____.

Ⓐ move in a happy and proud way

Ⓑ skip around in a big circle

Ⓒ walk slowly with your head down

Ⓓ glide along the floor like a snake

4. When you *scowl*, you show that you are ____.

Ⓕ angry

Ⓖ sorry

Ⓗ surprised

Ⓙ excited

Writing

Write about a kind act. Use **thoughtful** in your sentence.

_____

_____

drowsy

adjective

A **drowsy** person is very sleepy.

After a long day at the beach, Taylor felt so **drowsy** that she fell asleep on the car ride home.

What do people do when they are **drowsy**?

- They yawn.
- They prance around.
- They close their eyes.
- Their heads drop to their chests.
- They read long books.

When do you feel **drowsy**? How can people tell when you are **drowsy**?

glitter

verb

When something **glitters**, it shines and sparkles.

At the prince's ball, the ladies wore jewels that **glittered** in the candlelight.

Which things might **glitter**?

- a tennis shoe
- a diamond ring
- the stars at night
- a lake in the sunlight
- a peanut butter sandwich

Point out things in the classroom that **glitter**.
Do you have something at home that **glitters**?

pantomime

verb

You **pantomime** when you tell a story with movements and facial expressions rather than words.

There wasn't a sound as the kindergartners **pantomimed** how to make scrambled eggs.

Which of these could you **pantomime**?

- telling your name and address
- telling people you love them
- telling someone to quiet down
- telling people to stop
- telling what kind of dog you have

Show how you would **pantomime** to tell someone he or she did a good job.

selfish

adjective

A **selfish** person does not like to share.

The **selfish** girl would not share her toys with her sister.

Who is being **selfish**?

- Rodger will not let anyone play in his treehouse.
- Zelda gave me a taste of her sandwich.
- Ryan let Max choose a game to play.
- Luiz grabbed a handful of cookies and left two cookies for Ray.
- Carrie let me color with her brand-new crayons.

What is a **selfish** thing to do?
How could you persuade a **selfish** person to share toys with you?

drowsy • glitter • pantomime • selfish

Write on the board the four words studied this week. Read the words with the class and briefly review their meanings. Then conduct the oral activities below.

1 Tell students that you are going to give them a clue about one of the four words for the week. They are to find the word that answers the clue.

- This is a way to talk without words. **(pantomime)**

- This word describes someone who won't share. **(selfish)**

- This word describes someone who is ready for bed. **(drowsy)**

- Diamonds do this. **(glitter)**

2 Read each sentence and ask students to supply the correct word to complete the sentence.

- The baby gets ＿＿ when it's time for her nap. **(drowsy)**

- The lake's water will sparkle and ＿＿ in the sunlight. **(glitter)**

- Gordon was ＿＿ and took all of the new markers for himself. **(selfish)**

- It was so noisy on the playground that the teacher had to ＿＿ to tell her class to line up. **(pantomime)**

3 Read each sentence and ask students to tell which word or words are wrong. Then have them provide the correct word from the week's list.

- Maisie was wide-awake, so her eyes kept closing. **(wide-awake/drowsy)**

- The queen's diamond rings look dull in the sunlight. **(look dull/glitter)**

- Charlie was thoughtful when he grabbed the new crayons and left the broken ones for me. **(thoughtful/selfish)**

4 Read each sentence and ask students to decide if it is true or false. If the sentence is false, instruct students to explain why.

- Lakes and oceans glitter on gloomy days. **(false; water doesn't sparkle when the sun isn't shining on it)**

- When you pantomime, you might use a hand signal such as the thumbs-up sign. **(true)**

- *Selfish* has about the same meaning as *kind*. **(false; it isn't kind to behave selfishly)**

- A drowsy person needs sleep. **(true)**

Answers for page 119: 1. B, 2. J, 3. C, 4. F

Review Words	drowsy • glitter • pantomime • selfish

Fill in the bubble next to the correct answer.

1. Which means the opposite of *drowsy*?
- Ⓐ very sleepy
- Ⓑ wide-awake
- Ⓒ right on time
- Ⓓ very late

2. What did Connor do that was *selfish*?
- Ⓕ He shared his new toy trucks with his friend.
- Ⓖ He let his sister choose a movie for the two of them to watch.
- Ⓗ He offered to set the table for dinner.
- Ⓙ He did not give his brother a turn on the swing.

3. You could *pantomime* to ___.
- Ⓐ make a phone call
- Ⓑ talk to someone who is in another room
- Ⓒ show that you are sleepy
- Ⓓ call out for help

4. Which would *glitter* in the sun?
- Ⓕ a colorful jewel
- Ⓖ a rusty nail
- Ⓗ a pile of bricks
- Ⓙ banana slices

Writing

Write about feeling drowsy. Use **drowsy** in your sentence.

_____

_____

dwelling

noun

Your **dwelling** is the place where you live.

My uncle's **dwelling** has six rooms plus a basement where we play ping-pong.

Which materials do people use to build their **dwellings**?

- bricks
- wood
- bugs
- crayons
- stones

Tell about your **dwelling**.
Have you ever seen an animal's **dwelling**? What was it like?

bustle

verb

When you move with lots of energy, you **bustle**.

Before the family party, my parents **bustled** about the kitchen, cooking lots of good food.

Which words mean about the same as **bustle**?

- relax
- hurry
- rest
- rush
- keep busy

Tell about a time when you and your family **bustled** to get ready for a special day. How do you feel when you **bustle**?

react

verb

You **react** when you respond to something that happens.

I will **react** with a loud cheer and a big smile if my sister wins the race.

How would you **react** to these happenings?

- Your dog chews up your favorite book.
- Your picture is in the newspaper.
- You see a fat spider on your bed.
- You accidentally ripe your dad's jacket.
- A sudden clap of thunder shakes your house.

What are some ways that you **react** to good news?
What are some ways that you might **react** if your friend got hurt?

merry

adjective

A **merry** person is very happy and cheerful.

The **merry** girl smiled and laughed, and made everyone feel better.

What does a **merry** person do?

- dance
- laugh
- scowl
- clap
- cry

How would you pantomime to show that you are **merry**?
What makes you feel **merry**?

dwelling • bustle • react • merry

Write on the board the four words studied this week. Read the words with the class and briefly review their meanings. Then conduct the oral activities below.

1 Tell students that you are going to give them a clue about one of the four words for the week. They are to find the word that answers the clue.

- This is another word for *house*. **(dwelling)**

- You might feel this way on holidays. **(merry)**

- This is another word for *respond*. **(react)**

- People who are trying to get a lot done do this. **(bustle)**

2 Read each sentence and ask students to supply the correct word to complete the sentence.

- On the day before a trip, Mom and Dad ____ around, packing and loading the car. **(bustle)**

- My grandma will ____ with a smile when I give her these flowers. **(react)**

- Sarah's ____ is an apartment in a tall building in New York City. **(dwelling)**

- I can hear ____ laughter from the room next door. **(merry)**

3 Read each sentence and ask students to tell which word is wrong. Then have them provide the correct word from the week's list.

- "Joy" is a good name for my friend because she is always sad. **(sad/merry)**

- Marta moved to a new cave in the city. **(cave/dwelling)**

- We really had to creep about to get everything ready for the party. **(creep/bustle)**

4 Read each sentence and ask students to decide if it is true or false. If the sentence is false, instruct students to explain why.

- You hurry when you bustle. **(true)**

- A merry person is jolly. **(true)**

- One way to react to good news is to shout "Hooray!" **(true)**

- Everyone in the world lives in the same kind of dwelling. **(false; people live in different kinds of homes)**

Answers for page 123: 1. D, 2. G, 3. B, 4. H

Review Words dwelling • bustle • react • merry

Fill in the bubble next to the correct answer.

1. Who is *bustling*?

Ⓐ Katrina, who is reading a good book

Ⓑ Jack, who is taking a long nap

Ⓒ Matty, who is strolling down the street

Ⓓ Lee, who is hurrying to finish a job

2. Which word means about the same as *merry*?

Ⓕ mad

Ⓖ cheery

Ⓗ drowsy

Ⓙ lazy

3. How do most people *react* when their friends give them birthday gifts?

Ⓐ by saying "Happy birthday!"

Ⓑ by saying "Thanks!"

Ⓒ by saying "You're welcome!"

Ⓓ by saying "No, thanks!"

4. Which is a person's *dwelling*?

Ⓕ a tree branch

Ⓖ a shirt

Ⓗ a house

Ⓙ a stove

Writing

Write about a merry person. Use **merry** in your sentence.

_____

_____

pity

noun

You have **pity** when you feel sorry for someone.

Sam felt **pity** for the people who lost their homes when the hurricane hit.

Which sentences show **pity**?

- "I am so sorry that your dog got hit by a car."
- "You are too slow."
- "No one cares if you're hungry."
- "Let's collect food for the homeless."
- "Don't cry. I'll help you."

Tell about a time when you felt **pity** for someone. What did you say or do to show **pity**?

reduce

verb

When you **reduce** something, you make it smaller in size or amount.

We can't afford a new TV until the store **reduces** the price.

Which of the following can people **reduce**?

- the number of planets in space
- the amount of electricity they use at home
- their ages
- the amount of clutter they have at home
- the amount of money they spend

Tell about some ways to recycle and **reduce** waste at school.

jealous

adjective

When you want something that someone else has, you may feel **jealous**.

Marcy felt **jealous** when her friend got a bike like the one Marcy wanted.

Would you be likely to feel **jealous** if your friend:

- had a toothache?
- got a new skateboard?
- won a trip to Hawaii?
- lost his or her cat?
- had the flu?

Tell about a time when you felt **jealous**. What made you feel that way? How does it feel to be **jealous**?

hoarse

adjective

A **hoarse** voice sounds rough and weak.

Katie could not speak loudly because a bad cold had caused her voice to be **hoarse**.

What can make your voice **hoarse**?

- a sore throat
- a cough drop
- screaming when you're at a ballgame
- a good night's sleep
- talking for a long, long time

Have you ever had a **hoarse** voice? What made your voice **hoarse**? Make your voice sound **hoarse**.

pity • reduce • jealous • hoarse

Write on the board the four words studied this week. Read the words with the class and briefly review their meanings. Then conduct the oral activities below.

1 Tell students that you are going to give them a clue about one of the four words for the week. They are to find the word that answers the clue.

- We should do this to the amount of water we waste. **(reduce it)**

- You might feel this way if your friend won a trophy and you didn't. **(jealous)**

- This kind of voice can be hard to understand. **(hoarse)**

- You might have this feeling when you see a person with a broken leg. **(pity)**

2 Read each sentence and ask students to supply the correct word to complete the sentence.

- Mom gave me medicine to ____ my fever. **(reduce)**

- Trevor felt ____ when his friend Omar got his very own computer. **(jealous)**

- Heather felt ____ for the homeless cat, so she took it to a shelter. **(pity)**

- Jacob's sore throat made his voice sound ____. **(hoarse)**

3 Read each sentence and ask students to tell which word is wrong. Then have them provide the correct word from the week's list.

- My voice is strong from yelling and screaming on the roller coaster. **(strong/hoarse)**

- Wash your hands often to increase the chance of getting sick. **(increase/reduce)**

- Tess pouted because she was happy that Elena won the prize and she did not. **(happy/jealous)**

- My aunt felt silly when she saw the crying child looking for his mother, so she helped him search. **(silly/pity)**

4 Read each sentence and ask students to decide if it is true or false. If the sentence is false, instruct students to explain why.

- You might feel pity for a hurt dog. **(true)**

- A hoarse voice is strong and clear. **(false; a hoarse voice is weak and rough)**

- When people reduce their spending, they spend more money. **(false; to reduce spending means to spend less)**

- Jealous people feel merry. **(false; you don't feel happy when you're jealous)**

Answers for page 127: 1. D, 2. H, 3. A, 4. J

Name _____

Fill in the bubble next to the correct answer.

1. To *reduce* pollution means ___.
- Ⓐ to make more pollution
- Ⓑ to think about reasons for pollution
- Ⓒ to make pollution disappear forever
- Ⓓ to make less pollution

2. Which can become *hoarse*?
- Ⓕ your mouth
- Ⓖ your ears
- Ⓗ your voice
- Ⓙ your legs

3. What might a *jealous* child say to someone who won a bike?
- Ⓐ "It's not fair! I want that bike!"
- Ⓑ "I'm so happy that you won a bike!"
- Ⓒ "That's a great bike!"
- Ⓓ "Now we can ride bikes together."

4. If you feel *pity* for another person, you might ___.
- Ⓕ just walk away
- Ⓖ laugh at the person
- Ⓗ tell them to stop it
- Ⓙ try to help the person

Writing

Write about a person who feels pity. Use **pity** in your sentence.

_____

_____

abdomen

noun

Your **abdomen** is between your chest and hips. Your abdomen holds your stomach and other body parts.

He was breathing so deeply in his sleep that his **abdomen** was moving up and down.

Which of these body parts are in your **abdomen**?

- your skin
- your elbow
- your bellybutton
- your tongue
- your belly

Point to your **abdomen**.
Tell about a time when you had a pain in your **abdomen**. What caused the pain? What helped the pain go away?

occur

verb

Another way to say that things happen is to say they **occur**.

Snowstorms usually **occur** in the winter when it's cold.

Where would each of these events **occur**?

- playing on the bars
- eating breakfast
- checking out a book
- buying popcorn
- working math problems

Tell about something that **occurs** at night. Tell about something that **occurred** yesterday.

intense

adjective

Something that is **intense** is really strong.

I wore my sunglasses and a hat because the sunlight was **intense**.

Which of these words mean about the same as **intense**?

- weak
- strong
- young
- powerful
- merry

What are some kinds of **intense** weather? What problems can **intense** weather cause?

lack

verb

You **lack** something when you don't have it or you don't have enough of it.

Mrs. Harris **lacks** the money she needs to take a trip, so she will stay home.

What does a desert **lack**?

- lakes
- forests
- cactuses
- sand
- polar bears

What skills does a baby **lack**? What skills did you **lack** when you were in kindergarten?

abdomen • occur • intense • lack

Write on the board the four words studied this week. Read the words with the class and briefly review their meanings. Then conduct the oral activities below.

1 Tell students that you are going to give them a clue about one of the four words for the week. They are to find the word that answers the clue.

- This word names a part of your body. **(abdomen)**

- This kind of sunlight can give you a sunburn. **(intense)**

- This word means to be without. **(lack)**

- This word means to happen. **(occur)**

2 Read each sentence and ask students to supply the correct word to complete the sentence.

- The fire's ____ heat quickly toasted my marshmallow. **(intense)**

- My stomach growls when I ____ food. **(lack)**

- Mom gets a pain in the side of her ____ if she jogs right after she eats. **(abdomen)**

- A full moon will ____ at the end of the month. **(occur)**

3 Read each sentence and ask students to tell which word or words are wrong. Then have them provide the correct word from the week's list.

- The cats are very hungry because they have plenty of food. **(have plenty of/lack)**

- Your stomach is inside your head. **(head/abdomen)**

- Accidents never happen when people drive too fast. **(never happen/occur)**

- A tornado is a very gentle windstorm. **(gentle/intense)**

4 Read each sentence and ask students to decide if it is true or false. If the sentence is false, instruct students to explain why.

- If you lack a snack, you do not have one. **(true)**

- An intense rainstorm can cause a flood. **(true)**

- The abdomen is a part of the brain. **(false; the abdomen is located in the middle of the body)**

- When an event occurs, it ends. **(false; when an event occurs, it happens.)**

Answers for page 131: 1. D, 2. F, 3. B, 4. H

Review Words	abdomen • occur • intense • lack

Fill in the bubble next to the correct answer.

1. What does a bird *lack*?

Ⓐ wings

Ⓑ feet

Ⓒ feathers

Ⓓ teeth

2. Which is part of your *abdomen*?

Ⓕ your belly

Ⓖ your brain

Ⓗ your ankle

Ⓙ your back

3. What happens when cold weather grows more *intense*?

Ⓐ The weather warms up.

Ⓑ People put on warmer clothes.

Ⓒ People put on cooler clothes.

Ⓓ People go swimming at the beach.

4. When problems *occur*, they ____.

Ⓕ go away

Ⓖ get better

Ⓗ happen

Ⓙ get worse

Writing

Write about an intense storm. Use **intense** in your sentence.

_____

_____

befuddle

verb

Something that confuses you, **befuddles** you.

When two bells rang at the beginning of the school day, it **befuddled** the new student.

Which might **befuddle** you?

- Your friend uses a secret code to write you a message.
- Your teacher uses pantomime to tell a story.
- Your teacher asks you to read out loud to the class.
- You meet a new friend who does not speak the same language you speak.
- Your dad asks you to make your bed.

What **befuddles** you about the stars in the sky? What can you do when something **befuddles** you?

chum

noun

A **chum** is a good friend.

Gabe likes to sit next to his **chum** Aidan on the school bus.

Which words mean about the same as **chum**?

- pal
- buddy
- pet
- doctor
- friend

Tell what you like best about a **chum** of yours. How did you meet your **chum**?

demonstrate

verb

When you **demonstrate** something, you show how to do it.

The art teacher will **demonstrate** ways to make puppets.

Which could you **demonstrate** to a friend?

- how to tie shoelaces
- how to make cupcakes
- how to play a board game
- how to make a sock puppet
- how to eat with a knife, fork, and spoon

What game can you **demonstrate**? What would you need to **demonstrate** that game?

grateful

adjective

When you feel **grateful**, you feel thankful for the things that others give you or do for you.

Jed was **grateful** to his dad for fixing his bike.

How can you show that you are **grateful** for a gift?

- You can say, "Wow! Thanks!"
- You can say, "That's not what I wanted."
- You can write a thank-you note.
- You can say something nice about the gift.
- You can grab the gift and walk away.

Tell about a time when you felt **grateful** for something that someone did for you. What did that person do?
What is something you have that you are **grateful** for?

befuddle • chum • demonstrate • grateful

Write on the board the four words studied this week. Read the words with the class and briefly review their meanings. Then conduct the oral activities below.

1 Tell students that you are going to give them a clue about one of the four words for the week. They are to find the word that answers the clue.

- This is another word for *friend*. (**chum**)

- This word describes someone who feels thankful. (**grateful**)

- You do this when you show someone how to play a computer game. (**demonstrate**)

- Confusing ideas do this to people. (**befuddle them**)

2 Read each sentence and ask students to supply the correct word to complete the sentence.

- I'm so _____ to you for finding my lost dog and returning her to me. (**grateful**)

- Our guide will _____ how to paddle a canoe. (**demonstrate**)

- Read the clues carefully and the puzzle will not _____ you. (**befuddle**)

- My mom and her _____ see a movie together each month. (**chum**)

3 Read each sentence and ask students to tell which word or words are wrong. Then have them provide the correct word from the week's list.

- Megan and her enemy Molly promised to be friends forever. (**enemy/chum**)

- These confusing directions make everything clear to me. (**make everything clear to/befuddle**)

- Greg was angry that I helped him clean his room. (**angry/grateful**)

4 Read each sentence and ask students to decide if it is true or false. If the sentence is false, instruct students to explain why.

- You might want to share a secret with a chum. (**true**)

- People will be more willing to help you if you are grateful. (**true**)

- When something befuddles you, you understand it perfectly. (**false; it confuses you**)

- When you demonstrate something, you show others how to do it. (**true**)

Answers for page 135: 1. A, 2. G, 3. C, 4. H

Review Words	befuddle • chum • demonstrate • grateful

Fill in the bubble next to the correct answer.

1. When you *demonstrate* something, you ___.

Ⓐ show how to do it

Ⓑ ask how to do it

Ⓒ watch someone else do it

Ⓓ keep quiet about it

2. A person who is *grateful* is ___.

Ⓕ messy

Ⓖ thankful

Ⓗ upset

Ⓙ famous

3. A *chum* is a ___.

Ⓐ pillow

Ⓑ toy car

Ⓒ friend

Ⓓ song

4. When something *befuddles* you, you feel ___.

Ⓕ sure

Ⓖ grumpy

Ⓗ mixed-up

Ⓙ bored

Writing

Write about something you do with a chum. Use **chum** in your sentence.

_____

_____

mystery

noun

A **mystery** is something that people find hard to explain or understand.

I do not understand why a rainbow is curved. A rainbow is a **mystery** to me.

Which are **mysteries** to you?

- how dinosaurs died
- how old you will be in second grade
- how many stars there are in the sky
- the name of your school
- how your brain works

What **mysteries** do you wonder about? Do they have to do with animals, planets, or some other topic? How can you find answers to those **mysteries**?

slumber

verb

Slumber is another word for *sleep*.

My cat likes to **slumber** on a small, soft bed.

Which words mean about the same as **slumber**?

- nap
- dine
- lack
- snooze
- doze

If you have a pet, where does he or she like to **slumber**? Besides your bed, do you have a favorite place to **slumber**.

ample

adjective

When you have an **ample** amount of something, you have enough.

Our large yard has **ample** space for our dog to get the exercise she needs.

Which are **ample** meals for a hungry child?

- a green bean
- a chicken salad
- a glass of water
- a bowl of spaghetti and meatballs
- an oatmeal cookie

How much do you think is **ample** spending money for a six-year-old child?

What do you think is an **ample** amount of time for a first-grader to spend on homework?

question

verb

When you **question** someone, you ask that person something.

"Alex, how did you tear your shirt?" **questioned** my mom.

If you had a chance to **question** each of these people, what would you ask them?

- a child who lives in another country
- a worker who cares for elephants at a zoo
- your school principal
- a diver who goes deep into the ocean
- a person who creates masks and costumes

Why does a police officer **question** someone who might be a robber?

mystery • slumber • ample • question

Write on the board the four words studied this week. Read the words with the class and briefly review their meanings. Then conduct the oral activities below.

1 Tell students that you are going to give them a clue about one of the four words for the week. They are to find the word that answers the clue.

- This is what you do when you need to know something. **(question)**

- You usually wear pajamas to do this. **(slumber)**

- This word describes a good-sized meal. **(ample)**

- This word names something that is hard to figure out. **(mystery)**

2 Read each sentence and ask students to supply the correct word to complete the sentence.

- We had leftover food from the ____ dinner that Mom cooked. **(ample)**

- How fingernails grow is a ____ to me. **(mystery)**

- Tomas likes to ____ in a hammock that hangs between two trees. **(slumber)**

- My teacher likes to ____ us about each story we read. **(question)**

3 Read each sentence and ask students to tell which word or words are wrong. Then have them provide the correct word from the week's list.

- People run with their eyes closed. **(run/slumber)**

- Be sure to leave no food for the cat to eat while we're away. **(no/ample)**

- No one knows for sure why the dinosaurs died out—it is a simple reason. **(simple reason/mystery)**

- The principal will answer the students about the window they broke. **(answer/question)**

4 Read each sentence and ask students to decide if it is true or false. If the sentence is false, instruct students to explain why.

- You are wide-awake when you slumber. **(false; you are asleep when you slumber)**

- Mysteries are easy questions to figure out. **(false; they are hard to figure out)**

- Flowers need an ample amount of water to grow. **(true)**

- When you question someone, you are trying to find answers. **(true)**

Answers for page 139: 1. C, 2. H, 3. D, 4. G

| Review Words | mystery • slumber • ample • question |

Fill in the bubble next to the correct answer.

1. **When you have an *ample* amount of milk to drink, you have ____.**
   (A) way too much milk
   (B) no milk at all
   (C) as much milk as you need
   (D) not as much milk as you need

2. **Which of the following is a *mystery*?**
   (F) how old you are
   (G) how you got to school today
   (H) what job you will do when you grow up
   (J) what time it was when you woke up today

3. **Why might you *question* someone?**
   (A) to explain something to that person
   (B) to tell that person what your name is
   (C) to answer that person's questions
   (D) to get answers from that person

4. **Which do you do while you *slumber*?**
   (F) read
   (G) dream
   (H) play
   (J) eat

| Writing |

Write about a mystery that you wonder about. Use **mystery** in your sentence.

_____

_____

sympathetic

adjective

A **sympathetic** person is understanding of other people's problems and tries to help.

A **sympathetic** lady gave the hungry boy some food.

Who was **sympathetic**?

- Julie and Jess teased Austin about his new glasses.
- Darrin played with a new student who had no friends.
- Bart helped Charlie clean up the paint that Charlie spilled.
- Mom hugged me when I felt upset.
- Curt laughed when Walt dropped the ball.

When have you felt **sympathetic** with someone who was sad or hurt? What did you do to show that you were **sympathetic**?

tally

verb

When you **tally** numbers or things, you count them to find the total.

David will **tally** the scores to see which team won the game.

Why might you **tally** numbers of people or things?

- to see how many students are in the first grade
- to see if it is cloudy today
- to figure out what day it is
- to add up the runs scored in a baseball game
- to find how many students like cats best and how many like dogs best

Pretend we want to find out which ice-cream flavor is the class favorite. How would we **tally** to find the answer?

festive

adjective

Something that is **festive** is merry and cheerful.

We used clusters of red, yellow, and blue balloons to make the room look **festive**.

Which things can make a place look **festive**?

- streamers
- old shoes
- colored lights
- forks and spoons
- party hats

What would you wear to a party if you wanted to look **festive**?

voyage

noun

A **voyage** is a long trip to a faraway place.

My great-grandma took a **voyage** across the Pacific Ocean on a big ship.

Which of the following are **voyages**?

- a walk around the block
- a drive to the next town
- a trip to the moon
- a trip across an ocean
- a trip to the North Pole

Pretend you are going on a **voyage**. Where will your **voyage** take you? Can you find that place on a map?

sympathetic • tally • festive • voyage

Write on the board the four words studied this week. Read the words with the class and briefly review their meanings. Then conduct the oral activities below.

1 Tell students that you are going to give them a clue about one of the four words for the week. They are to find the word that answers the clue.

- This is a trip to a faraway place. (**a voyage**)

- A room looks this way when you decorate it for a party. (**festive**)

- This word describes someone who cares about others. (**sympathetic**)

- You might do this when you add numbers to find a score. (**tally**)

2 Read each sentence and ask students to supply the correct word to complete the sentence.

- We have boat tickets for a ____ to the South Pole. (**voyage**)

- Our waiter will ____ the cost of the food we ate to see how much money we owe. (**tally**)

- I used pretty ribbons to make the birthday gift look ____. (**festive**)

- My ____ teacher took me to the school nurse when I bumped my head. (**sympathetic**)

3 Read each sentence and ask students to tell which word is wrong. Then have them provide the correct word from the week's list.

- This summer, I am taking a walk from the United States to China. (**walk/voyage**)

- A mean girl brought the thirsty child some water. (**mean/sympathetic**)

- Balloons, streamers, and confetti make a room look boring. (**boring/festive**)

- I will erase the scores to see who is the winner. (**erase/tally**)

4 Read each sentence and ask students to decide if it is true or false. If the sentence is false, instruct students to explain why.

- Bright colors usually look more festive than dull ones. (**true**)

- A sympathetic person ignores others when they're sad. (**false; a sympathetic person is kind to others**)

- You count when you tally numbers. (**true**)

- No one brings suitcases on voyages. (**false; most people bring suitcases on long trips**)

Answers for page 143: 1. B, 2. H, 3. D, 4. F

Review Words   sympathetic • tally • festive • voyage

Fill in the bubble next to the correct answer.

1. Which sentence uses the word *tally* correctly?

Ⓐ I will tally Joseph to see if he can come over to play.

Ⓑ Jan will tally the votes to see who won the election.

Ⓒ Let's tally a coin to see who will go first.

Ⓓ My cat is hungry, so please tally her.

2. A *sympathetic* person is ____.

Ⓕ drowsy

Ⓖ jealous

Ⓗ thoughtful

Ⓙ wealthy

3. How long might a *voyage* last?

Ⓐ a few hours

Ⓑ a few minutes

Ⓒ one day

Ⓓ weeks

4. A room looks *festive* when it is ____.

Ⓕ decorated for a party

Ⓖ messy and cluttered

Ⓗ full of old sofas and chairs

Ⓙ neat, clean, and empty

Writing

Write about a festive event. Use **festive** in your sentence.

_____

_____

method

noun

A **method** is the way you do something.

Mom's **method** for cleaning the house is to dust first and then vacuum.

What is a **method** for:

- washing a car?
- getting ready for bed?
- learning a song?
- getting dressed for school?
- eating corn on the cob?

What is your **method** for doing your homework?

object

verb

When you **object**, you do not agree.

Luke **objects** to going to bed at 8:00 on a school night.

Would you **object** if you were told:

- all children must wear striped pajamas to school?
- all children must eat a healthy breakfast?
- all children must do 4 hours of homework every night?
- all children must ride elephants to school?
- all children must be kind?

What is a rule that you **object** to? What are your reasons for **objecting** to that rule?

thrill

verb

Something **thrills** you when you feel great excitement.

The thought of one day getting to fly to outer space **thrills** me.

Which ones **thrill** you?

- a parade
- a ride on a roller coaster
- the sound of a fire engine
- hearing someone say that you're wonderful
- car races

What do you do that **thrills** you? What do some people do that seems to **thrill** them, but seems too scary to you?

cooperative

adjective

A **cooperative** person works well with other people.

I love having **cooperative** teammates who play well together.

Would you be **cooperative** if you:

- took turns while playing a game?
- said "I quit"?
- listened when others spoke?
- helped with a school project?
- cheated so that you could win?

Tell about a time when you were **cooperative** in the classroom.

method • object • thrill • cooperative

Write on the board the four words studied this week. Read the words with the class and briefly review their meanings. Then conduct the oral activities below.

1 Tell students that you are going to give them a clue about one of the four words for the week. They are to find the word that answers the clue.

- A helicopter ride might do this to you. **(thrill you)**

- Your parents do this when they do not want you to do something. **(object to it)**

- This is a way to do something. **(a method)**

- This word describes people who work nicely together. **(cooperative)**

2 Read each sentence and ask students to supply the correct word to complete the sentence.

- It will ____ me to see a whale when we're out on the ocean. **(thrill)**

- The ____ group members listened carefully and worked well together. **(cooperative)**

- Lisa's ____ for washing her dog is to put the dog in the shower. **(method)**

- I know that my dad will ____ if I ask to see a movie on a school night. **(object)**

3 Read each sentence and ask students to tell which word is wrong. Then have them provide the correct word from the week's list.

- Since I don't like purple, I agree to painting the house that color. **(agree/object)**

- Sasha was selfish and helped everyone in her group. **(selfish/cooperative)**

- The skateboarders bore me when they speed down the ramps and then turn upside down. **(bore/thrill)**

4 Read each sentence and ask students to decide if it is true or false. If the sentence is false, instruct students to explain why.

- Something that thrills you is very exciting. **(true)**

- It is hard to work with a cooperative person. **(false; a cooperative person works well with others)**

- One method for cooking chicken is to bake it. **(true)**

- You object when you do not agree with something. **(true)**

Answers for page 147: 1. C, 2. G, 3. A, 4. J

Name _____

Fill in the bubble next to the correct answer.

1. Which word means about the same as *thrill*?
- Ⓐ bore
- Ⓑ teach
- Ⓒ excite
- Ⓓ learn

2. When you are *cooperative,* you ____.
- Ⓕ work alone
- Ⓖ work well with others
- Ⓗ want to be the boss
- Ⓙ always think that you are right

3. When you *object* to a decision, you ____.
- Ⓐ do not agree with it
- Ⓑ agree with it
- Ⓒ are not sure about it
- Ⓓ do not care about it

4. Which sentence tells about a *method*?
- Ⓕ Alexander has a large collection of toy cars.
- Ⓖ This book is full of beautiful pictures.
- Ⓗ This ladybug is bright orange with two black dots.
- Ⓙ I sit at the kitchen table to do my homework.

Writing

Write about your method for keeping dry on rainy days. Use **method** in your sentence.

_____

_____

Dictionary

Aa

abdomen • *noun*

Your abdomen is between your chest and hips. Your abdomen holds your stomach and other body parts.

He was breathing so deeply in his sleep that his abdomen was moving up and down.

aim • *noun*

Your aim is a goal that you are willing to work for.

My aim for the weekend is to finish building my model boat.

ample • *adjective*

When you have an ample amount of something, you have enough.

Our large yard has ample space for our dog to get the exercise she needs.

appreciate • *verb*

When you appreciate something, you are thankful for it.

I appreciate the movies you gave me to watch while I was sick.

Bb

bashful • *adjective*

Someone who is bashful feels shy, especially around new people.

The new student was so bashful that she looked down when the teacher introduced her.

befuddle • *verb*

Something that confuses you, befuddles you.

When two bells rang at the beginning of the school day, it befuddled the new student.

boast • *verb*

When you boast, you talk with too much pride about yourself.

We were tired of hearing Casey boast about the home run he hit.

breeze • *noun*

A breeze is a light and gentle wind.

A cool breeze feels good on a hot day.

bustle • *verb*

When you move with lots of energy, you bustle.

Before the family party, my parents bustled about the kitchen, cooking lots of good food.

busybody • *noun*

A busybody is nosy and wants to know everyone else's business.

Ana is a busybody who stands close to me and tries to hear everything I say to my friend.

Cc

chatter • *verb*

When you chatter, you talk about things that are not important.

Dad and his friends often chatter about the kinds of cars they like.

chum • *noun*

A chum is good friend.

Gabe likes to sit next to his chum Aidan on the school bus.

clever • *adjective*

A clever person is smart and can quickly figure things out.

The clever police officer looked at the clues and figured out who had robbed the store.

cluster • *noun*

A cluster is a number of things of the same kind that grow or are grouped close together.

Mom tucked a small cluster of green grapes into my lunchbox.

cluttered • *adjective*

A cluttered place is messy and full of things.

The drawer is so cluttered that I can't find a pencil.

collection • *noun*

A collection is a group of things that are alike.

Emily has large and small seashells in her shell collection.

compete • *verb*

People who compete take part in contests, sports, or games.

I am going to compete in a spelling bee to win a big trophy.

cooperative • *adjective*

A cooperative person works well with other people.

I love having cooperative teammates who play well together.

create • *verb*

You create something when you make it from your own ideas.

I want to create a puppet using paper plates, colored paper, crayons, and glue.

creep • *verb*

People who creep move carefully and quietly so that no one will see or hear them.

My brother likes to creep up behind me when I'm reading a book. Then he says "Boo!"

crunch • *verb*

When you crunch, you chew noisily on something.

I could hear my brother crunch his potato chips.

Dd

damp • *adjective*

A damp object is a little bit wet.

My dog does not like baths, so I use a damp towel to clean her.

dangle • *verb*

Something dangles when it hangs down and swings loosely.

When I dangle a piece of yarn in front of my cat, she jumps up and grabs it.

daring • *adjective*

A daring person is brave and tries adventuresome things.

My daring brother learned how to skydive.

dash • *verb*

When you dash, you move quickly.

I must dash to the supermarket before it closes.

dazzle • *verb*

You dazzle people when you amaze and impress them.

The ice skater dazzled the audience when she jumped into the air and twirled around.

deed • *noun*

When you do a good deed, you do something nice for someone.

My mom said I did a good deed when I let my little sister play with my friend and me.

demonstrate • *verb*

When you demonstrate something, you show how to do it.

The art teacher will demonstrate ways to make puppets.

dine • *verb*

When you dine, you eat dinner.

My family usually dines at our kitchen table around six o'clock at night.

direct • *verb*

When you direct someone, you tell that person how to get somewhere.

Can you please direct me to the principal's office?

discuss • *verb*

People discuss something when they talk about it.

Let's discuss the best places to visit when we go on our family vacation.

dismiss • *verb*

When you dismiss people, you let them leave.

Mr. Powell will dismiss us from school when the bell rings.

dodge • *verb*

You dodge something by quickly getting out of its way.

I had to dodge a beach ball that was flying toward my head.

drenched • *adjective*

Something is drenched when it is soaking wet.

My shoes were drenched from playing in rain puddles on my way home from school.

drowsy • *adjective*

A drowsy person is very sleepy.

After a long day at the beach, Taylor felt so drowsy that she fell asleep on the car ride home.

dull • *adjective*

Something that is dull is boring.

Harry thinks books without pictures are dull.

dwelling • *noun*

Your dwelling is the place where you live.

My uncle's dwelling has six rooms plus a basement where we play ping-pong.

Ee

entrance • *noun*

The entrance is the way into a place.

A car blocked the entrance to the school parking lot.

equipment • *noun*

Equipment is a set of special things you need for a particular activity.

A tent and sleeping bags are some of the equipment we need to go camping.

explore • *verb*

When you explore, you learn about something new.

David wants to explore the cave so he can see the strange animals that live inside it.

Ff

famous • *adjective*

A famous person is someone whom most people know about or recognize.

The crowd clapped and cheered when the famous singer rode by in the parade.

favor • *noun*

A favor is something nice that you do for another person.

The busy teacher said, "Please do me a favor and pass out the pencils."

festive • *adjective*

Something that is festive is merry and cheerful.

We used clusters of red, yellow, and blue balloons to make the room look festive.

fetch • *verb*

When you fetch, you go and get something.

My mom asked me to fetch her car keys from the kitchen table.

final • *adjective*

Something that is final comes at the end.

We will go home early on the final day of school.

firm • *adjective*

A firm object is hard and solid.

I know that this apple is firm because it feels hard when I press my thumb on it.

flabbergasted • *adjective*

A flabbergasted person is surprised and amazed.

April was flabbergasted when she opened the door and heard everyone yell "Surprise!"

flutter • *verb*

Something flutters when it quickly flaps up and down or from side to side.

A butterfly flutters its wings when it flies.

focus • *verb*

You focus when you pay attention.

Lucy could not focus on her homework because her brother was playing loud music.

frisky • *adjective*

A frisky animal or person is playful and lively.

The frisky puppy dashed wildly around the yard in circles.

fuss • *noun*

You make a fuss to show that you are upset about something.

Sam argued and made a fuss because he didn't want to wear gloves and a scarf to school.

Gg

garment • *noun*

A garment is a piece of clothing.

Kelly likes to play dress-up and wear a garment that is too big for her.

gentle • *adjective*

A gentle person is careful not to hurt people or things.

The gentle teacher spoke softly to the upset child and dried his tears.

giggle • *verb*

When you giggle, you laugh in a silly or nervous way.

The girls at the sleepover giggled as they put makeup on each other.

glance • *verb*

When you glance at something, you look quickly at it.

Before we leave for school, Mom glances at me to see if my hair is combed.

glitter • *verb*

When something glitters, it shines and sparkles.

At the prince's ball, the ladies wore jewels that glittered in the candlelight.

gloomy • *adjective*

Someone who is gloomy feels sad.

Ben felt gloomy after his dog ran away from home.

gnaw • *verb*

You gnaw on something when you chew on it again and again.

My dog loves to gnaw on toy bones I buy at the pet store.

grateful • *adjective*

When you feel grateful, you feel thankful for the things that others give you or do for you.

Jed was grateful to his dad for fixing his bike.

grouchy • *adjective*

A grouchy person is in a bad mood.

My little brother is grouchy when he doesn't get enough sleep.

Hh

handy • *adjective*

Something that is handy is useful.

A backpack is a handy bag for carrying things to school.

harbor • *noun*

A harbor is a place next to the land where ships and boats are kept.

The ship sailed into the harbor, where it would be safe from the storm.

hero • *noun*

A hero is a person who does a brave and good thing.

That firefighter is the hero who saved the boy from the burning house.

hoarse • *adjective*

A hoarse voice sounds rough and weak.

Katie could not speak loudly because a bad cold had caused her voice to be hoarse.

hobby • *noun*

A hobby is something that you like to do for fun.

On Saturdays, Mark enjoys his hobby of building wooden birdhouses.

horrible • *adjective*

Something that is horrible is very bad.

I had a horrible cold that made my head ache, my nose run, and my throat sore.

hush • *verb*

When you hush, you become quiet.

Our teacher asked everyone to hush so she could read us a story.

Ii

intense • *adjective*

Something that is intense is really strong.

I wore my sunglasses and a hat because the sunlight was intense.

interest • *noun*

You have an interest in something if you want to know more about it.

When he was my age, my dad showed an interest in playing the guitar.

Jj

jabber • *verb*

When you jabber, you talk fast and make little sense.

When Ryan gets excited, he often jabbers so fast that we can't understand him.

jealous • *adjective*

When you want something that someone else has, you may feel jealous.

Marcy felt jealous when her friend got a bike like the one Marcy wanted.

jolly • *adjective*

A jolly person is happy and full of fun.

My jolly Aunt Meg likes to laugh and have a good time.

jumbo • *adjective*

Something that is jumbo is very big.

The jumbo burger at Fred's Burger House is big enough for three people.

L l

lack • *verb*

You lack something when you don't have it or you don't have enough of it.

Mrs. Harris lacks the money she needs to take a trip, so she will stay home.

M m

merry • *adjective*

A merry person is very happy and cheerful.

The merry girl smiled and laughed, and made everyone feel better.

method • *noun*

A method is the way you do something.

Mom's method for cleaning the house is to dust first and then vacuum.

mighty • *adjective*

A mighty person or thing is strong and powerful.

The lion gave a mighty roar that shook the leaves on the trees.

mystery • *noun*

A mystery is something that people find hard to explain or understand.

I do not understand why a rainbow is curved. A rainbow is a mystery to me.

N n

nature • *noun*

Nature is everything in the world that is not made by people, such as trees, rocks, and animals.

Our drive through the forest gave us a chance to enjoy the beauty of nature.

nibble • *verb*

You nibble your food when you eat it in small bites.

My pet mouse nibbled on a piece of cheese.

nimble • *adjective*

A nimble person or animal moves quickly and easily.

The nimble goat jumped from rock to rock without slipping.

nutritious • *adjective*

Nutritious food has vitamins and other things that you need to stay healthy.

Fresh fruits and vegetables are nutritious foods that people should eat every day.

O o

object • *verb*

When you object, you do not agree.

Luke objects to going to bed at 8:00 on a school night.

occur • *verb*

Another way to say that things happen is to say they occur.

Snowstorms usually occur in the winter when it's cold.

odd • *adjective*

Something is odd if it is strange or unusual.

A penguin is an odd bird because it does not fly.

odor • *noun*

An odor is a smell.

Skunks have a strong odor that can be smelled from far away.

P p

panic • *verb*

When you panic, you become very afraid and don't know what to do.

The people inside the elevator began to panic when the door would not open.

pantomime • *verb*

You pantomime when you tell a story with movements and facial expressions rather than words.

There wasn't a sound as the kindergartners pantomimed how to make scrambled eggs.

patient • *adjective*

A patient person does not get upset when things take a long time.

The patient teacher repeated the directions over and over until everyone knew what to do.

pause • *verb*

You pause when you stop what you are doing for a short time.

Let's pause for lunch and then finish our work when we come back.

peer • *verb*

You peer when you look very hard at something to see it better.

Sean peered into the aquarium full of fish and tried to find the tiny snail.

peppy • *adjective*

A peppy person or animal is full of energy.

My peppy baby sister jumped up and down in her crib.

permit • *verb*

You permit something when you allow it to happen.

Will you permit me to go to the beach with Sam and his family?

pest • *noun*

A pest is someone or something that really bothers you.

Ants can be pests when they walk all over our picnic food.

pity • *noun*

You have pity when you feel sorry for someone.

Sam felt pity for the people who lost their homes when the hurricane hit.

poky • *adjective*

Someone or something that moves slowly is poky.

Sometimes my dog is poky on walks because she stops to smell everything she sees.

popular • *adjective*

If a thing is popular, many people like it.

Dogs and cats are popular pets in many places around the world.

prance • *verb*

When you prance, you move around happily and proudly.

Andy began to prance around the field after he scored the winning goal for his soccer team.

prefer • *verb*

You prefer something when you like it better than other things.

Annie prefers chocolate ice cream to vanilla.

present • *verb*

To present means to show or introduce something.

The circus ringmaster called out to the crowd, "I now present the Great Bandini!"

Qq

question • *verb*

When you question someone, you ask that person something.

"Alex, how did you tear your shirt?" questioned my mom.

Rr

racket • *noun*

A racket is a lot of very loud noise.

The squawking birds in the pet store made an awful racket.

react • *verb*

You react when you respond to something that happens.

I will react with a loud cheer and a big smile if my sister wins the race.

reduce • *verb*

When you reduce something, you make it smaller in size or amount.

We can't afford a new TV until the store reduces the price.

regret • *verb*

You regret something when you are sorry about it.

I regret calling my friend a name that made him cry.

ridiculous • *adjective*

Something that is very silly is ridiculous.

It would be ridiculous to wear polka-dotted pajamas to school.

rustle • *verb*

Things rustle when they rub together and make a soft crackling sound.

When a breeze blows through a tree, its leaves rustle.

Ss

sample • *noun*

A sample is a small amount of something that shows what the rest is like.

Michael asked for a sample of rocky-road ice cream so he could find out if he liked the flavor.

scamper • *verb*

Something scampers when it runs quickly and lightly.

My cat watches squirrels scamper up and down an oak tree.

scowl • *verb*

When you scowl, you make an angry frown.

My mom and dad scowl whenever I tease my little brother.

screech • *noun*

A screech is a loud, high-pitched noise that may sound scary.

When the car stopped suddenly, its brakes made a screech.

scrub • *verb*

To scrub something, you rub it very hard to clean it.

I will have to scrub that pot because there is burned food stuck inside it.

selfish • *adjective*

A selfish person does not like to share.

The selfish girl would not share her toys with her sister.

sensible • *adjective*

Sensible people think carefully and make wise choices.

Austin decided that it wouldn't be sensible to walk across the frozen pond.

shiver • *verb*

When you shiver, you shake because you are cold or afraid.

When I got out of the swimming pool, the cold wind made me shiver.

skill • *noun*

A skill is the ability to do something well.

Playing the piano is a skill that takes a lot of practice.

slumber • *verb*

Slumber is another word for *sleep*.

My cat likes to slumber on a small, soft bed.

snicker • *verb*

When you laugh in a mean way, you snicker.

When her stepmom told Cinderella she could not go to the ball, Cinderella's stepsisters snickered.

sniff • *verb*

When you sniff, you take short breaths through your nose.

Sniff this shampoo and tell me if you like the way it smells.

snoop • *verb*

You snoop when you sneak a look at something.

I snooped under Mom and Dad's bed to see if my birthday presents were hidden there.

soar • *verb*

Birds and planes soar when they glide or fly high in the sky.

Eagles sometimes soar through the air without flapping their wings.

speck • *noun*

A speck is a small spot or a small mark.

You can hardly see it, but there is a speck of red ink on my white shirt.

splendid • *adjective*

Something that is splendid is beautiful or magnificent.

The splendid sunset splashed the sky with pink, orange, and purple streaks.

strange • *adjective*

Something that is strange is odd or unusual.

We all stared at the strange sight of a man walking down the street on his hands.

stroll • *verb*

When you stroll, you take a slow, relaxed walk.

Gina likes to take her time and stroll past the animals when she goes to the zoo.

swift • *adjective*

Something that is swift moves very quickly.

A swift wind quickly blew the sailboats out to sea.

sympathetic • *adjective*

A sympathetic person is understanding of other people's problems and tries to help.

A sympathetic lady gave the hungry boy some food.

Tt

tally • *verb*

When you tally numbers or things, you count them to find the total.

David will tally the scores to see which team won the game.

tame • *adjective*

Something that is tame is gentle and not wild.

The tame deer were not afraid to be near us.

task • *noun*

A task is a small job or chore.

My sister's task is to set the table for dinner.

texture • *noun*

Texture is the way something feels or looks.

A baby's skin has a soft, smooth texture like rose petals.

thoughtful • *adjective*

A thoughtful person thinks about other people's feelings and needs.

It was so thoughtful of you to make me a get-well card when I was sick.

thrill • *verb*

Something thrills you when you feel great excitement.

The thought of one day getting to fly to outer space thrills me.

tour • *noun*

When you go somewhere interesting, you can take a tour of that place to learn more about it.

My family took a tour of a movie studio to see how movies are made.

V v

vehicle • *noun*

People ride in vehicles and use them for moving things.

Cars, buses, bicycles, and trains are kinds of vehicles that go on land.

victory • *noun*

When you win, you gain a victory.

The soccer players yelled "Victory!" after their team won the championship game.

voyage • *noun*

A voyage is a long trip to a faraway place.

My great-grandma took a voyage across the Pacific Ocean on a big ship.

W w

wander • *verb*

You wander when you walk around without a purpose or a plan.

Jake decided to wander around the mall until it was time for the movie to start.

wavy • *adjective*

A wavy line has curves and is not straight.

My skirt has wavy lines that go up and down like ocean waves.

wealthy • *adjective*

A wealthy person has a lot of money.

Our wealthy neighbors own three cars, two boats, and a house on an island.

wiggle • *verb*

You wiggle when you twist and turn from side to side in a jerky way.

It's fun to wiggle when you dance.

wild • *adjective*

A wild animal is not tame and lives in nature.

A lion is a wild animal that lives on grasslands and hunts for its food.

Y y

yelp • *verb*

You yelp when you cry out quickly and sharply in pain.

The puppy yelped when Chris accidentally stepped on its paw.

Z z

zip • *verb*

When something zips, it moves fast.

The antelope zipped across the plain to escape the hungry lion.

Index